Resort & Sports English

Myeong-Hee Seong
Katie Mae Klemsen

BAEKSAN Publishing Co.

SCOPE AND SEQUENCE

CHAPTER

I

Resort Hotels

UNIT 1 Be Our Guest

Unit Goals

- Introduce vocabulary and conversation skills for living and working in resorts
- Practice practical resort-specific English
- Learn about jobs and facilities associated with resorts
- Develop reading comprehension skills with career-relevant articles
- Preview global resort careers and popular resort destinations

Vocabulary

- Conflicting
- Compensation
- Neighbor
- Booming
- To break into
- Personnel
- Functional
- Enthusiastic
- To take off
- World-class
- Amenities
- Laid back
- Refurbishment
- To harmonize
- Stunning
- Shutter
- Balcony
- Nocturnal
- Swaths

Let's Get Started

Translate these common questions relating to general resort knowledge. Resort staff would ask some questions, and guests would ask others. In the blank provided, write the letter "S" for staff or the letter "G" for guest, indicating who would ask the question.

1. Is this an all-inclusive resort? ____

2. Would you like a ski-in / ski-out room? ____

3. Is this a luxury resort? ____

4. How many guests will accompany you? ____

5. Would you like a translator? ____

6. When does the bar close? ____

7. Is this beach private? ____

8. When would you like your tennis lesson? ____

9. Would you like a facial or manicure today? ____

10. Is the restaurant here public or private? ____

Conversation I

Seung Jae: I have always wanted to work in a resort. Did you know that?

Dawn: No way! Me, too, but I have heard a lot of conflicting information about resorts.

Seung Jae: What have you heard, for example?

Dawn: Well, I get the impression there are many types of resorts, and they specialize in different leisure activities. I'm just not sure where to start looking for the perfect resort job.

Seung Jae: Dawn, very few things are perfect. But I think I know what you mean. There are a lot of considerations to make.

Dawn: Tell me about it; I have considered location, amenities, compensation packages, resort style, position and career development opportunities.

Seung Jae: Wow, you really have considered nearly everything. What's your next move?

Dawn: I need to do some research. I need to find out about resort styles and locations. I should decide which department and faculty I would like to work in. Then I will research which resorts are hiring.

Seung Jae: Looks like you have a lot of work to do.

Dawn: Sure. Sometimes good things aren't easy, and easy things aren't good. Haven't you heard that saying before?

Conversation II

Seung Jae: So, I was researching about working at ski resorts. Wouldn't that be great?

Dawn: Not really, Seung Jae. I hate the cold.

Seung Jae: Well, speak for yourself. I learned to ski when I was 3 years old. I would kill for a job at a ski resort.

Dawn: I much prefer warm weather. That's why I have been looking into beach resorts.

Seung Jae: Guess we won't be neighbors anymore. But hey, who says we can't visit each other every so often?

Dawn: That sounds like a plan. I think I want to work in Indonesia though. Bali sounds like it has great working conditions.

Seung Jae: Korean tourism is booming there. I think you might have a lot of opportunities. You should go for it.

Dawn: Thanks for the support. What about you? Where would you like to work?

Seung Jae: Europe has world-class resorts, but I might intern at a ski resort in Japan first. Experience counts a lot these days. For the best chance at employment, I really want to have an internship.

Dawn: You're right. Internships are truly valuable. I should look into that, too. It's a great way to build skills and gain experience.

Conversation III

Seung Jae: I've been reading about career opportunities in resorts lately. Which area are you looking into?

Dawn: Me? I've been looking at guest relations. I think that I'm good with people, so that might work well for me. What about you?

Seung Jae: I would like to work in the food services department. I think managing a restaurant would be fantastic.

Dawn: You have to know a lot about food services. Are you ready for that?

Seung Jae: Well, not just yet, but many resorts have great management training programs that help employees to gain promotion within the company.

Dawn: Planning a career is a smart move. It's ideal to consider the long-term now. Planning is an important part of success.

Seung Jae: Well said, Dawn. What is your plan for breaking into guest relations?

Dawn: Good question. I'm working on it.

Seung Jae: What have you learned so far?

Dawn: First, personnel should be multi-lingual, so I am enrolling in an advanced Japanese class. This way I will be functional in Korean, English and Japanese.

Seung Jae: Wonderful. That's a terrific idea. Continuing education shows you're serious about the career. Good for you.

Conversation IV

Seung Jae: Hey, Dawn. What's up?

Dawn: Not much, but did you hear about the job opening in China?

Seung Jae: No. What's it for?

Dawn: It's at the new golf resort on Hainan Island.

Seung Jae: Oh. Great.

Dawn: That doesn't sound very enthusiastic. I thought you would be excited. It sounds great. It's a world-class luxury resort. It's right up your alley.

Seung Jae: Sure, perfect, except for the fact that it's a GOLF resort. I hate golf.

Dawn: Hate is a strong word; what's your problem with it?

Seung Jae: Golf is for old people. It's super boring. I can't imagine a life like that.

Dawn: Are you kidding me? Have you been sleeping for the past 5 years? Golf has seriously taken off. It's not for the old and boring. Have you ever even been golfing?

Seung Jae: No. But . . .

Dawn: There are no excuses. That's it. You're coming with me. I have a lesson with a pro golfer this afternoon at the driving range. If you hate it after an hour, fine. But I think you'll be surprised. You should never judge a book by its cover.

Resorts

What is a resort? Who goes there? What facilities are available? What careers are available in resort tourism management? There are many questions associated with resort tourism and careers. Read about the many types of resorts below.

A resort is a place used for relaxation or recreation, attracting visitors for holidays or vacations. Resorts are places, towns or commercial establishments operated by a single company. Such a self-contained resort attempts to provide for most of a vacationer's wants while remaining on the premises, such as food, drink, lodging, sports, entertainment, and shopping. The term "resort" may also be used to identify a hotel property that provides an array of amenities and typically includes entertainment and recreational activities.

Destination Resorts

A destination resort is a resort that contains the necessary guest attraction capabilities and does not need to be near a destination, town, historic site, or theme park, to attract the guests. A commercial establishment at a resort destination such as a recreational area, a scenic or historic site, a theme park, a gaming facility or other tourist attraction may compete with other businesses at a destination. Consequently, another characteristic of a destination resort is that it offers food, drink, lodging, sports, entertainment, and shopping within the facility so that guests have no need to leave the facility throughout their stay.

All-Inclusive Resorts

An all-inclusive resort is a resort that, besides providing all of the common amenities of a resort, charges a fixed price that includes most or all items. At a minimum, most inclusive resorts include lodging, unlimited food, drink, sports activities, and entertainment for the fixed price. In recent years, the number of resorts offering "all-inclusive" amenities has decreased dramatically; in 1961, over half offered such plans and in 2007, less than ten percent did.

Spa Resorts

A spa resort is a short-term residential or lodging facility with the primary purpose of providing individual services for spa-goers to develop healthy habits and relax while on holiday. Historically, many such spas were developed at the location of natural hot springs or sources of mineral waters. Typically, over a seven-day stay, such facilities provide a comprehensive program that includes spa services, physical fitness activities, wellness education, healthy cuisine and special interest programming.

Golf Resorts

Golf resorts are resorts that cater specifically to the sport of golf, and include access to one or more golf course and or clubhouse. Golf resorts typically provide golf packages that provide visitors with all greens and cart fees, range balls, accommodations and meals. Pro lessons and access to golf-specific shopping can all be arranged.

Ski Resorts

A ski resort is a ski area plus amenities that generally make them a destination resort. This includes accommodations and other amenities adjacent to the ski area. Some ski resorts offer lodging options on the slopes themselves, with ski-in and ski-out access allowing guests to ski right up to the door. Ski resorts often have other activities, such as snowmobiling, sledding, horse-drawn sleds, dog-sledding, ice-skating, indoor or outdoor swimming, spas, game rooms, and local forms of entertainment, such as clubs and cinema.

Beach Resorts

Beach resorts are located on a coast. Many seaside towns have turned to other entertainment industries, and some of them have a good deal of nightlife. The cinemas and theatres often remain to become host to a number of pubs, bars, restaurants and nightclubs. Most of their entertainment facilities cater to local people and the beaches still remain popular during the summer months. A host of the best beach resorts in the world are in Thailand, Malaysia, and Indonesia; in Korea's back yard.

Luxury Resorts

A luxury resort is an expensive vacation facility, which is fully staffed and has been highly rated, usually by an international or national travel association. Luxury resorts often boast many visitor activities and attractions such as golf, water sports, spa and beauty facilities, skiing, natural ecology and tranquility. Because of the extent of amenities offered, a luxury resort is also considered a destination resort.

Megaresorts

A Megaresort is a type of destination resort which is of an exceptionally large size, sometimes featuring large-scale attractions, such as casinos and gambling facilities, golf courses, theme parks, and multiple accommodations. The hotels and casinos along the Las Vegas Strip are often considered megaresorts due to their immense size and complexity.

Concepts

Answer the following questions from the information provided in this unit.

1. What is the difference between an all-inclusive resort and a destination resort? How are they similar? How are they different?

2. Where would you go if you wanted a relaxing vacation where you could receive a variety of beauty treatments? Does more than one type of resort address this?

3. What is a megaresort and how is it different from a luxury resort?

4. What type of resort is Disneyland?

5. Name three resorts. What type of resort are they?

Further Reading

The Best Beach Resorts In The World

Looking for the ultimate beach getaway? Want to find that perfect stretch of beach and blue water where you can let all your cares drift away on warm tropical breezes? Welcome to the Forbes.com list of the best beach resorts in the world. Many countries, of course, can offer many fine resorts, but to make your decision easier, we have picked only one resort per country, based on the beauty of the beach and the service and amenities of the resort. Whether you are looking for a family-oriented vacation or a romantic getaway, chances are you will find the resort that's right for you.

Hayman, Australia

Anyone who has seen the northeast coast of Australia can see its one long stretch of some of the finest beach in the world. The weather is so mild and Australians are so laid back that many people don't even bother staying in a hotel and just sleep on the beach. But if you are looking for something more luxurious, there is no finer resort in Queensland than Hayman. Located in the famous Great Barrier Reef (home of some of the best scuba diving in the world) and near Whitsunday Island, the hotel has just undergone a two-year, $15 million refurbishment that should more than justify the amount of traveling you'll have to do to get here.

The Datai, Malaysia

Set between rainforest and ocean, the Datai is a sleek, modern resort that has been designed not so much to stand out against, but to harmonize with its environment. From a main hotel building, individual guest villas radiate out like branches from a great tree, all connected by covered open-air walkways that allow guests to feel part of the surrounding jungle. In addition to its long white sand beach, the resort has an 18-hole championship golf course and a spa.

Amanpuri, Thailand

Phuket is one of the greatest beaches in the world, and the Amanpuri is its finest resort. Barefoot, smiling staff greets you on arrival and usher you to your own private bungalow decorated in traditional Thai style, with beautiful fabrics and woodwork, and a deck with views of the silent blue surf. The name Amanpuri means peace, and the name is appropriate. Everything is done to make life as relaxed and peaceful as possible for guests. From the spa to the beach to the restaurants, the staff seem truly dedicated to making your stay here as comfortable as possible.

Four Seasons Resort Bali at Jimbaran Bay, Indonesia

One has to hand it to the Four Seasons people--they know what it takes to run a top-of-the-line resort. Jimbaran Bay may just be the jewel in their considerable crown. Maybe it's the low cost of labor or real estate in Bali, maybe it's the natural friendliness of the Balinese, maybe it's stunning beauty of the place, and maybe it's just something they put in the water, but with its traditional thatch-roofed villas, abundance of flowers, superb food, world-class spa and beautiful beaches, Jimbaran Bay is about as perfect a romantic luxury beach resort as you could want to find.

Shutters on the Beach, The United States of America

Although it only opened in 1993, Shutters on the Beach calls to mind a grand resort hotel of the 1920s. Each one of its nearly 200 rooms have shuttered doors that open onto private balconies but guests who want to have a view of the ocean will have to pay more. The hotel has become a favorite romantic getaway for the Hollywood crowd, and is the only luxury beachfront hotel in Los Angeles.

Hotel Splendido, Italy

Portofino is one of the great summer playgrounds of Europe, and the Hotel Splendido is at its very heart. Many of the wealthiest families in Italy summer here in their own villas or stop by in their yachts, and it is easy to see why. The harbor is both picturesque and perfect for the kind of water sports that Italians love: waterskiing and speedboat racing. Nocturnal sports are just as much fun, though, and the town's discos and nightclubs stay open well into the morning. Positioned overlooking the harbor, the Splendido, a former private villa, is at once part of it all and wonderfully removed. You can come here and dance until dawn or just relax and let the superb staff pamper you.

Hôtel du Cap--Eden Roc, France

Hotel du Cap on the French Riviera has been one of the most storied and luxurious resorts in the world. Visitors should not expect to find the wide swaths of beach that they might in the Caribbean--the beach in fact is quite small and rocky, like most in the south of France--but what they will find is incomparable elegance bordering on opulence. Situated on a 22-acre private peninsula jutting out into the Mediterranean, the hotel is famous for favoring celebrities and the very wealthy--which seem to comprise most of the guests. Everything here is first class and commensurately pricey.

The Marbella Club, Spain

The Marbella Club is not a misnomer. Although anyone who can afford it can stay here, it's clear from the moment you arrive that many of the people here seem more comfortable than just regular guests. That's because the resort has been drawing wealthy Europeans and their families for decades. Many actually grew up coming here for holidays throughout the year. This, plus the lush tropical gardens that surround and fill the resort and hide it from the outside world, gives it an unmistakable and well-deserved air of exclusivity. Besides the beach, there is a new 18-hole golf course, a Thalassotherapy spa, fine dining, a great poolside bar, paddle tennis and, at night, some of the best discos and nightclubs in Spain.

Practice Makes Perfect

1. Answer the following questions related to the article. Use complete sentences for your answer.

1) Why do you think Shutters on the Beach, in California, was named so?

2) Which resort is located on a 22-acre private peninsula? What amenities are found at that resort?

3) Which resort could you recommend for someone who wants a romantic vacation? What architectural features are found at that resort? What other things is the resort famous for?

4) Which resort harmonizes with the environment? Which type of natural environment is the resort located in?

5) At which resort can you expect the staff members to be barefoot? What is your opinion on this matter?

2. Match the following words from the previous article to the definition that best matches. Draw a line to connect the matching pairs.

1) Drift •	• A) Services
2) Amenities •	• B) To compliment
3) Laid back •	• C) Terrace
4) Refurbishment •	• D) A long, narrow piece of something
5) Harmonize •	• E) A window cover
6) Stunning •	• F) Relaxed
7) Shutter •	• G) Dramatic
8) Balcony •	• H) Of the night
9) Nocturnal •	• I) Renovation
10) Swath •	• J) To float

3. Use the following word in a sentence.

1) Laid back: ______________________________

2) Swath: ______________________________

3) Drift: ______________________________

Just Do It

Verbs are the parts of speech that indicate action. Phrasal verbs are two-word verbs, prepositional verbs or two verbs used together. Review the two phrasal verbs below.

To cough something up

- To produce something by means of giving, vomiting or coughing.

EXAMPLE:

- The dog coughed up the rabbit.
- The man finally coughed up the money he owed.

To break up

- To fall apart or end a relationship, or to begin to laugh a lot.

EXAMPLE:

- I broke up with my boyfriend.
- The comedian was so funny that the audience broke up.

UNIT 2 First Impressions

Unit Goals

- Build vocabulary and conversation skills for guest reservations, recommendations and the concierge desk
- Practice practical resort-specific English
- Learn to make guest recommendations
- Develop reading comprehension skills with career-relevant articles

Vocabulary

- Reservation
- Conference
- Particular
- Alternate
- To book
- Additional
- Bistro
- Quaint
- Sightseeing
- Historical
- Convenient
- To discover
- Prosthetic
- Limb
- To mislay
- To donate
- Charity
- Blow-up
- To recover
- Dentures

Let's Get Started

Translate these common questions relating to the Front Desk of a resort. Resort staff would ask some questions, and guests would ask others. In the blank provided, write the letter "S" for staff or the letter "G" for guest, indicating who would ask the question.

1. How may I help you? ____

2. Do you have a reservation? ____

3. Can I see your passport? ____

4. How long will you be staying? ____

5. Can I get a wakeup call please? ____

6. Is tax included? ____

7. What time is checkout? ____

8. Does the room have an Internet connection? ____

9. Does the room have a view? ____

10. Is breakfast included? ____

Conversation I

Seung Jae: Hello, Park Shore Resort, my name is Seung Jae, how may I help you?

Dawn: Hi, Seung Jae. I would like to make a reservation, please.

Seung Jae: No problem. When would you like to visit?

Dawn: Do you have a single room available on June 26th for 4 nights?

Seung Jae: Just one moment while I check those dates.

Dawn: Okay.

Seung Jae: Miss? I am sorry, but we are fully booked during those dates. Do you have alternate dates in mind?

Dawn: Are there any double rooms available? I can't be flexible on the dates. I am visiting to attend a conference, and I have to be there during that particular time.

Seung Jae: Will you be attending the Golf Show Conference?

Dawn: Exactly.

Seung Jae: Then I have good news. Our resort has reserved several rooms for the conference guests at a special price.

Dawn: That's fantastic. Should I give you my name and personal information for the reservation then?

Seung Jae: Yes, please. Go ahead whenever you are ready.

Conversation II

Seung Jae: Hello, Park Shore Resort, my name is Seung Jae, how may I help you?

Dawn: I would like to book a room, please.

Seung Jae: Sure. When would you like it?

Dawn: On April 7th, please.

Seung Jae: And what type of room would you like? We have beautiful suites available that overlook the garden.

Dawn: That won't be necessary. I would like a double room for two people.

Seung Jae: Perfect. How many nights would you like to reserve the room for?

Dawn: I would like to stay for 2 nights.

Seung Jae: Can I please have your name?

Dawn: My name is Dawn Marie. First name Dawn; D-A-W-N. Last name Marie; M-A-R-I-E.

Seung Jae: Thanks. I would like to confirm then, a double room for two guests, on April 7th for 2 nights. Also, you would like one additional blanket in the room.

Dawn: Yep. That's it.

Seung Jae: Great. I am looking forward to your arrival, Ms. Marie. See you on the 7th.

Conversation III

Seung Jae: Hello, Ms. Marie. How are you today?

Dawn: I am great, thanks, but I would like to do some sightseeing today.

Seung Jae: That sounds like a great idea. What would you like to see?

Dawn: I heard that downtown was full of interesting buildings and parks. Is that true?

Seung Jae: Yes, the historical district of the city has many museums and parks you can enjoy.

Dawn: What should I see first?

Seung Jae: I recommend the Classical Chinese Garden. It is a beautiful place to enjoy a quiet walk, enjoy classical architecture, and a freshly brewed tea.

Dawn: That sounds wonderful.

Seung Jae: Will you be needing your car today?

Dawn: Yes, I would like to drive there, unless there is a convenient bus service to the garden.

Seung Jae: Actually, Ms. Marie, there is a bus that will pick you up just outside of the resort's main gate. Three stops from here it will drop you off in front of the Chinese Garden.

Dawn: Well, then no need to call for the car.

Seung Jae: Have a great day, and please enjoy the garden on such a beautiful day.

Conversation IV

Seung Jae: Ms. Marie, did you enjoy the garden?

Dawn: Yes, Seung Jae, it was perfect. Thank you for the recommendation.

Seung Jae: Have you eaten dinner?

Dawn: No, not yet. I was hoping you could recommend somewhere to eat, too.

Seung Jae: It would be my pleasure. What would you like this evening?

Dawn: I was thinking about something simple, like a bistro or deli even.

Seung Jae: There is a quaint place called the Flying Elephant that has great salads, soups and sandwiches. How does that sound?

Dawn: It's just what the doctor ordered. Sounds perfect.

Seung Jae: Would you like a city map? I can circle the location of the deli on the map for you, if you like.

Dawn: Sure. It's better to be safe than sorry. Or, rather, better to have a map than get lost and be hungry.

Seung Jae: That's a great way to look at it. The map will also help you tomorrow, if you decide to explore the city more.

Dawn: Thanks again for your help. I don't know what I would do without you.

A Job Well Done

Review the job descriptions below for front office personnel.

The Front Office

The front office is considered the 'nerve center' of a resort. A warm, professional and an efficient front desk staff will set the tone right for a perfect guest experience. Read the jobs descriptions associated with the front desk below.

Front Office Manager (FOM)

The Front Office Manager is responsible for all duties of the front desk operation, which includes: staff training, inter-department communications, and staff scheduling. The FOM usually works a regularly scheduled front desk shift and must be available to work any shift as needed. The Front Office Manager should possess strong communication skills and demonstrate leadership abilities.

Concierge

The concierge is available to answer any guest inquires regarding the city, events, and attractions. This individual will provide exceptional customer service to all of our guests and will support other departments including Sales, Front Office, and Bellman, as needed.

Guest Service Agent

Guest Service Agents are responsible for greeting and registering the guest, providing outstanding guest service during their stay, and settling the guest's account upon completion of their stay. However, the realm of responsibilities will extend beyond that of a typical front desk agent. Primary responsibilities include: registering guests, making and modifying reservations, hotel operator, and concierge duties. Guest Service Agents must possess a positive and upbeat personality with a desire to deliver outstanding customer service to our guests.

Night Auditor

Night Auditors are responsible for the front desk operation during the overnight shift. Primary responsibilities include: registering guests, making reservations, preparing daily reports, balancing transactions, and conducting security walks. Night Auditors must be able to work independently and with minimal supervision. They must also be able to problem solve and troubleshoot in order to resolve guest issues that may arise and respond to emergency situations.

Security

The Security position will encompass aspects of both the Night Audit and Front Desk positions as well as overseeing the safety and security of the hotel and guests throughout the evening hours. Additional responsibilities include: conducting security walks throughout the resort property and responding to guest requests and any noise complaints. Security agents must be able to problem solve and troubleshoot in order to resolve guest issues and respond appropriately to emergency situations.

Van Driver

Van Drivers are responsible for transporting guests to and from the hotel to local area attractions as well as assisting the guest with recommendations for restaurants and tourist activities. The Van Driver is also expected to support with front desk operations. Primary responsibilities include: driving guests to designated locations, assisting guests with luggage, maintaining vehicle cleanliness, and concierge duties. Van Drivers must have strong analytical and navigation skills with the ability to coordinate multiple pick-ups and drop-offs on a schedule under continuously changing circumstances. A valid driver's license and acceptable driving record is required.

Concepts

Answer the following questions from the information provided in this unit.

1. What are the primary responsibilities of the front desk manager?

2. What is the difference between Night Auditor and Security?

3. What does it mean to say that the front desk is the "nerve center" of a hotel?

4. What are the duties of the Van Driver?

5. What is the primary role of the concierge desk?

Further Reading

Left Behind

Have you ever gone on vacation and returned home, only to discover that you left something behind in your hotel? If you answered yes, you are not alone. Hotel guests in England seem to be leaving behind more and more items each year. Absent-minded guests managed to leave prosthetic limbs behind, as well as a blow-up sheep. They also mislaid a printer, crutches and dentures according to a survey by Holiday Inn Other items recovered from rooms have included £2,000 in cash, a Gucci watch, and a monk fancy dress outfit.

Hotel managers reported that around £2.5 million worth of items are left behind each year, with phone chargers and underwear the most-recovered things.

Each year, hotel employees find:

42,000 phone chargers worth around £630,000;
40,000 items of underwear worth around £200,000;
14,000 toothbrushes worth around £21,000;
11,500 pairs of glasses worth around £1.15 million;
5,000 hair-straighteners worth around £500,000.

Jane Bednall, from Holiday Inn, said: “It's quite unbelievable just how much is left behind by our guests each year. The phone chargers would easily stretch across the English Channel. She also stated that most of the items are not re-claimed. People simply replace the forgotten items once they return home. After a waiting period of six months anything of value is donated to local charities.

Practice Makes Perfect

1. Answer the following questions related to the article. Use complete sentences for your answer.

1) What is the estimated value of all of the phone chargers left in hotel rooms?

2) Name three odd items that have been left in hotel rooms in England.

3) How long do the hotels save the items before getting rid of them?

4) Where do the forgotten items go to once the waiting period is over?

5) Have you ever left anything in a hotel room? What was it? Where did you leave it?

2. Match the following words from the previous article to the definition that best matches. Draw a line to connect the matching pairs.

1) Discover •	• A) An arm or leg
2) Prosthetics •	• B) To lose or misplace
3) Limb •	• C) To give, rather than to sell
4) Mislay •	• D) Fake teeth used to replace lost teeth
5) Donate •	• E) To find after misplacing or losing
6) Charity •	• F) Inflatable
7) Blow-up •	• G) False, unnatural
8) Absent-minded •	• H) To find for the first time
9) Recover •	• I) Forgetful
10) Dentures •	• J) For the aid and assistance of others

3. Use the following word in a sentence.

1) Donate: ____________________

2) Discover: ____________________

3) Recover: ____________________

Just Do It

Verbs are the parts of speech that indicate action. Phrasal verbs are two-word verbs, prepositional verbs or two verbs used together. Review the two phrasal verbs below.

To turn something in

- To submit something, usually an article or be-longing, to someone, usually an individual or group, especially someone in charge.

EXAMPLE:

- The good citizen turned in the wallet which he had found in the park.

To make something up

- To create something, or invent something

EXAMPLE:

- Instead of telling the truth, the customer made his story up.

UNIT 3

Eat It Up

Unit Goals

- Build vocabulary and conversation skills for restaurant guest relations
- Practice practical resort-specific English
- Learn about job associated with food services
- Develop reading comprehension skills with career-relevant articles

Vocabulary

- Host
- Immediately
- Meantime
- Soft–boiled
- Hard–boiled
- Sourdough
- Cashier
- Unfortunately
- Dessert
- Availability
- Local
- Handful
- Locavore
- To establish
- Versatile
- Seasonal
- To stomp
- Partnership
- Distributor
- To harvest

Let's Get Started

Translate these common questions relating to the food services in a resort. Resort staff would ask some questions, and guests would ask others. In the blank provided, write the letter "S" for staff or the letter "G" for guest, indicating who would ask the question.

1. Are you ready to order? ____

2. What kind of tea do you have? ____

3. How would you like your steak cooked? ____

4. Can I have the check, please? ____

5. Would you like a dessert menu? ____

6. How is your meal? ____

7. Can I get a table for four? ____

8. Do you have any recommendations? ____

9. What sides would you like? ____

10. How would you like your eggs? ____

Conversation I

Seung Jae: Good evening. Do you have a reservation tonight?

Dawn: Yes, as a matter of fact, I do. It's under the name "Dawn."

Seung Jae: Yes, here it is. That's a reservation for four?

Dawn: Yes, but there will actually be five tonight.

Seung Jae: Very well, let me check the table availability.

Dawn: Sure. Can you please seat us at a table near the window? I would love to enjoy the sunset tonight.

Seung Jae: Yes, Ms. Marie. Please follow me.

Dawn: Can you get me a glass of water, please?

Seung Jae: Actually, Steve will be your host tonight. I will send him to your table immediately.

Dawn: Thank you.

Conversation II

Dawn: I would like a table for two, please.

Seung Jae: Do you have a reservation tonight?

Dawn: No, I just arrived, and didn't call ahead.

Seung Jae: I'm sorry, but we are full for dinner service.

Dawn: Really? I wasn't expecting this. Is there anything you can do?

Seung Jae: Let me see. It looks like I can have a table for you in about 25 to 30 minutes. Are you willing to wait?

Dawn: A short wait is no problem.

Seung Jae: Why don't you take a seat at the bar and we can get your drink order in the meantime.

Dawn: That sounds great. Thanks for working us in.

Seung Jae: It's my pleasure.

Conversation III

Seung Jae: Good morning. How are you today?

Dawn: Good morning. I am well, thank you.

Seung Jae: Would you like to see the menu?

Dawn: No, thanks. I think I am ready to order.

Seung Jae: Great. What can I get for you?

Dawn: I would like the American breakfast, please.

Seung Jae: Coffee or tea?

Dawn: Coffee, please.

Seung Jae: And how would you like your eggs?

Dawn: What are my options?

Seung Jae: You can order them scrambled, fried, soft-boiled, hard-boiled, or sunny side up.

Dawn: Scrambled eggs would be great.

Seung Jae: Would you like toast or hash browns?

Dawn: Toast, please. What kind of bread do you have?

Seung Jae: We have white, wheat, sourdough, bagels and English muffins.

Dawn: Sourdough will be fine. Thanks.

Seung Jae: Perfect. That's one American breakfast with coffee, scrambled eggs, and sourdough toast. It will be right out.

Conversation IV

Seung Jae: How is your meal today?

Dawn: It's fantastic. Thanks for recommending the special. I really enjoyed it.

Seung Jae: Yes, it is very good. Will there be anything else today?

Dawn: No, I am afraid I am far too full for dessert.

Seung Jae: Shall I bring your bill?

Dawn: Yes, please. (Seung Jae brings the bill)

Seung Jae: Take your time. I will be your cashier when you are ready.

Dawn: Can I use a credit card?

Seung Jae: Yes, we accept Visa, Mastercard, and American Express.

Dawn: I have Diners Club. Is that okay?

Seung Jae: Unfortunately, we do not accept that card. Do you have another you would like to use today?

Dawn: I'll use my Visa. Here you go. Thanks.

A Job Well Done

Review the job descriptions below for resort food service personnel.

Food Services

Resort food service is complex, with many departments under Food and Beverage. There are restaurants, room service, beverage, banquets and kitchen, all reporting to the Director of Food Services. Unlike the majority of foodservice operations, resort foodservice works with other departments within resorts: housekeeping for linen, human resources for hiring, and purchasing to get approval for purchase orders before placing orders to vendors. Read the jobs descriptions associated with food services below.

Director of Food Services

The director of food service is responsible for the overall performance of the department. This includes the financial and service aspects of resort dining. The director must hire and train food service staff, develop, implement and monitor quality insurance standards, and create the working schedule for the staff. The successful director will also show creativity in developing programs to attract resort guests, and review customer satisfaction reports.

Continental Breakfast Attendant

The Continental Breakfast Attendant is responsible for setting up the daily complimentary continental breakfast, ensuring that the breakfast items are well stocked, and cleaning up after breakfast. This position requires multi-tasking abilities and ability to effectively communicate with guests regarding breakfast offerings and basic hotel information. A valid Food Handler's permit is required.

Bartender

Bartenders fill drink orders that waiters and waitresses take from customers. They prepare standard mixed drinks and, occasionally, are asked to mix drinks to suit a customer's taste. Most bartenders know dozens of drink recipes and are able to mix drinks accurately, quickly, and without waste, even during the busiest periods. Besides mixing and serving drinks, bartenders collect payment, operate the cash register, clean up after customers leave, and often serve food to customers seated at the bar. Bartenders also check identification of customers seated at the bar, to ensure they meet the minimum age requirement for the purchase of alcohol and tobacco products. Bartenders usually are responsible for ordering and maintaining an inventory of liquor, mixes, and other bar supplies.

Hosts and Hostess

Hosts and hostesses try to create a good impression of a restaurant by warmly welcoming guests. Because hosts and hostesses are restaurants' personal representatives, they try to insure that service is prompt and courteous and that the meal meets expectations. They may courteously direct patrons to where coats and other personal items may be left and indicate where patrons can wait until their table is ready. Hosts and hostesses assign guests to tables suitable for the size of their group, escort patrons to their seats, and provide menus. They also schedule dining reservations, arrange parties, and organize any special services that are required. In some restaurants, they also act as cashiers.

Dining Room Attendant

These attendants assist waiters, waitresses, and bartenders by cleaning tables, removing dirty dishes, and keeping serving areas stocked with supplies. They replenish the supply of clean linens, dishes, silverware, and glasses in the dining room and keep the bar stocked with glasses, liquor, ice, and drink garnishes. Bartender helpers also keep bar equipment clean and wash glasses. Dining room attendants set tables with clean tablecloths, napkins, silverware, glasses, and dishes and serve ice water, rolls, and butter. At the conclusion of meals, they remove dirty dishes and soiled linens from tables.

Concepts

Answer the following questions from the information provided in this unit.

1. How is the food services department dependant on other departments within a hotel or resort?

2. In Conversation I, Dawn says, "tonight we will be 5." To what is she referring?

3. How is a host different from a dining room attendant?

4. What is a continental breakfast?

5. Why should food service staff enforce local and national laws regarding food safety?

Further Reading

Hotels Take 'Locally Grown' a Step Beyond

David Garcelon, a chef, says he enjoys checking on the little strawberries, spinach, mint and several varieties of grapes in his small garden. But he is not out in his backyard; he's on the 14th-floor roof of the Fairmont Royal York in Toronto, where the view is of the steel, glass and concrete of nearby skyscrapers.

"You can just grab a handful of ripe tomatoes and they're ready to add to a dish for a small lunch for a board meeting," said Mr. Garcelon, executive chef of the hotel. "It is a much more interesting way to eat. It is almost inevitably fresher and better."

Eating local, homegrown cuisine is not new. There are plenty of practicing "locavores," and restaurants have been serving fresh, local food for a while. But now, hotels are "going local," establishing partnerships with area farmers and growing food in rooftop gardens as they begin to cater to travelers seeking to eat healthily on the road. Nor are the hotels' efforts limited to growing fruits and vegetables. Some hotels are now keeping bees, whose honey sweetens tea and soups, desserts and cocktails.
"There is almost not a more versatile product," Mr. Garcelon said. The hotel installed hives in 2008, and last year harvested about 450 pounds of honey.

Mariano Stellner, a corporate director of food and beverage for the hotel's parent, Fairmont Hotels & Resorts, said the company encouraged its chefs to "stay local, stay seasonal, whenever possible."

The number of hotels with working gardens and bees is quickly rising, said Bjorn Hanson, divisional dean of the Preston Robert Tisch Center for Hospitality, Tourism and Sports Management at New York University. "It is kind of the ultimate version of local," he said. "It creates a positive image, and people will pay a premium for it."

The Chicago Marriott Downtown Magnificent Mile has a garden, too. But it also cures its own meats, makes its own cheeses and pastas, and even stomps grapes in the lobby, and with guests' help, they create wines, said Myk Banas, executive chef and director of food and beverage operations. "If you order macaroni and cheese, we make the macaroni, and we make the cheese and the cheese sauce."

The hotel also has bees in its ninth-floor rooftop garden, and some of the honey is used in Rooftop Honey Wheat Beer, made in partnership with a local brewery. "It is so local, it's only sold on one block," Mr. Banas said.

Some hotels do not have their own gardens but establish close relationships with nearby farms. "We change our dinner menu up until 5 p.m., depending on what products we get," said Jason McLeod, the executive chef the Elysian Hotel in Chicago, which opened in December. It is more difficult than ordering everything through one distributor; because the hotel deals with a number of local farms, he said, "on some nights, we call 20 to 30 farms to place orders."

The hotel has gone one step further by reserving land at Heritage Prairie Farm in Elburn, Ill., to grow produce specifically for the hotel, and to keep its bees. On a recent visit to the farm, the culinary team, which included bartenders and servers, planted seeds for tomatoes used for its homemade ketchup. The staff also sometimes assists with the harvests at farms. "You have to commit fully," Mr. McLeod said. "We're very passionate about what we do."

Practice Makes Perfect

Reading Comprehension

1. Answer the following questions related to the article. Use complete sentences for your answer.

1) What is a locavore?

2) How is the hotel restaurant industry changing the way people eat?

3) Who is Myk Banas? If a guest orders macaroni and cheese from his kitchen, what does he make himself?

4) Why do hotels now have to build relationships with local farms? What role is the local farm playing the hotel restaurant industry?

5) How much honey does the hotel produce last year?

2. Match the following words to the definition that best matches. Draw a line to connect the matching pairs.

1) Local	•	• A) A person that gives something out, dispenses it
2) Handful	•	• B) All-purpose and very useful
3) Establish	•	• C) A person that eats what is grown locally
4) Versatile	•	• D) To begin, start or create
5) Seasonal	•	• E) To gather
6) Stomp	•	• F) A small amount of something
7) Partnership	•	• G) A group or joint effort in something
8) Harvest	•	• H) Regionally limited
9) Locavore	•	• I) To smash, usually with the feet
10) Distributor	•	• J) According to the time of year

3. Use the following word in a sentence.

1) Local: ____________________

2) Harvest: ____________________

3) Handful: ____________________

Just Do It

Verbs are the parts of speech that indicate action. Phrasal verbs are two-word verbs, prepositional verbs or two verbs used together. Review the two phrasal verbs below.

To beat oneself up

• To be critical of one's behavior or actions.

EXAMPLE:

• After making a major mistake I usually beat myself up.

To wear out

• To become worn from use.

EXAMPLE:

• The stove in the kitchen is worn out.

UNIT 4 Running a Tight Ship

Unit Goals

- Build vocabulary and conversation skills for housekeeping and resort maintenance
- Practice practical resort-specific English
- Learn about jobs associated with housekeeping and resort maintenance
- Develop reading comprehension skills with career-relevant articles

Vocabulary

- Bedding
- Starch / to starch
- To shrink
- Briefcase
- Straps
- Business cards
- Thermostat
- Fahrenheit
- Celsius
- Inconvenience
- Voucher
- To sleuth
- Conclusively
- Sympathy
- To mention
- Windowsill
- To light up
- Ledge
- Paper trail
- Evidence

Let's Get Started

Translate these common questions relating to the maintenance of a resort. Resort staff would ask some questions, and guests would ask others. In the blank provided, write the letter "S" for staff or the letter "G" for guest, indicating who would ask the question.

1. Do you offer room service? ____

2. When would you like to pick up your laundry? ____

3. Can you please fix the leaky faucet? ____

4. Can I provide you with additional toiletries? ____

5. Can you please bring me two more towels? ____

6. Can you leave dirty towels on the floor? ____

7. Can you clean my room every two days, please? ____

8. Is the air conditioner working yet? ____

9. Is that loud noise from room construction? ____

10. Can you please put tissue in the bathroom in the lobby? ____

Conversation I

Seung Jae: Housekeeping. How may I help you?

Dawn: Hi. This is Ms. Marie, in room 1004.

Seung Jae: Yes, Ms. Marie, how can I assist you today?

Dawn: I requested an extra blanket in my room when I checked in, and it's not here. Can you please bring one for me?

Seung Jae: Ms. Marie, did you check the closet for the extra blanket? Sometimes housekeeping puts the extra bedding there.

Dawn: Okay, give me one moment to check. (She checks for the blanket.) No, it's not there.

Seung Jae: I'm so sorry about that. I will have someone send one immediately.

Dawn: I would appreciate that. Thank you.

Seung Jae: Have a good day, Ms. Marie.

Dawn: You, too.

Conversation II

Seung Jae: This is laundry service. How may I help you?

Dawn: I sent my clothes to be washed this morning, and I forgot to tell you something.

Seung Jae: Let me find your service request. What is your name?

Dawn: This is Dawn Marie, room 1004.

Seung Jae: Yes, here is the request. What additional instructions would you like to leave?

Dawn: Please, I do not want any starch on my shirts. Also, don't wash my clothing in hot water. I do not want anything to shrink.

Seung Jae: Of course. I will add those notes right away. What time would you like to get the laundry?

Dawn: Can you leave it in my room tomorrow, when housekeeping cleans? I would like to have it early.

Seung Jae: Yes, I will do that. Anything else today?

Dawn: No, that will be all. Thank you.

Seung Jae: Have a great day.

Conversation III

Seung Jae: Hello, Ms. Marie. How can I help you?

Dawn: Well, I can't find my briefcase. I thought I had it in the lobby before breakfast, but I can't be sure. I think I have lost it.

Seung Jae: I see. Can you describe it for me, and I will see if I can help you find it.

Dawn: It's made of black leather and it has long, thin carrying straps.

Seung Jae: Do you have any identification inside?

Dawn: My business cards are inside, so it should be easy to know if it is mine.

Seung Jae: Ok. I will call the lost and found office, and let our security know to be on the look out. Can I get your cell number to call you when I find it?

Dawn: My phone is in the briefcase.

Seung Jae: I will call your room. 1004, right?

Dawn: Yes, and thank you for the help. It's urgent. I really need my briefcase.

Seung Jae: I completely understand. I will call you as soon as I have any information.

Conversation IV

Seung Jae: This is Seung Jae. How can I help you?

Dawn: I am calling from room 1004. My room is very cold, even with my extra blanket. I think there might be a problem with the thermostat.

Seung Jae: Is it set to 70 degrees?

Dawn: I'm sorry, I am not familiar with Fahrenheit. What is that in Celsius?

Seung Jae: Seventy degrees Fahrenheit is about 21 degrees Celsius.

Dawn: Yes, the thermostat says 22 degrees, but it feels like 16. It's so cold.

Seung Jae: Yes, it sounds like a problem. Let me call maintenance and send someone to look at it for you.

Dawn: Please do so quickly. It's quite uncomfortable in here now.

Seung Jae: Certainly. I will do it right away.

Dawn: Thank you. Have a good evening.

Seung Jae: You're welcome and I apologize for any inconvenience this has caused you.

A Job Well Done

Review the job descriptions below for housekeeping and maintenance personnel.

Housekeeping and Maintenance

In resorts, a major part of revenue comes from rooms. Rooms that are not sold create a profit loss for the resort. These rooms may not sell because of many factors, but many times the cleanliness of the room is a priority. Guests spend more time alone in a room than in any other area of the resort. Guests may check for dust, etc. and might lose confidence if the work is not properly done. The housekeeping department contributes greatly to the overall guest impression of the resort.

Resort maintenance workers, while not often seen, are an important sector of the total staff that keeps a resort running smoothly. Resort maintenance jobs are needed to deal with everything from stopped-up drains to malfunctioning television sets and burned out light bulbs. Larger properties employ specialists for plumbing, and electrical responsibilities, while smaller resorts often employ one or two maintenance workers who are adept at all the trades.

Housekeeping

Executive Housekeeper

The Executive Housekeeper is responsible for all duties of the housekeeping operation and cleanliness levels in all areas of the property. Responsibilities include: staff training, inter-department communications, and staff scheduling. The Executive Housekeeper will promote an atmosphere that insures the company mission statement, "Friendliness and Cleanliness". This position requires strong attention to detail, leadership skills, and the ability to effectively deal with department heads, guests, and team members.

Assistant Executive Housekeeper

The Assistant Executive Housekeeper supports the Executive Housekeeper in all duties of the housekeeping operation and cleanliness levels in all areas of the property. Responsibilities include: staff training, inter-department communications, and staff scheduling. The Assistant Executive will promote an atmosphere that insures the company mission statement, "Friendliness and Cleanliness". This position requires strong attention to detail, leadership skills, and the ability to effectively deal with department heads, guests, and team members.

Houseperson

The Houseperson is responsible for maintaining the cleanliness and appearance of the resort and providing customers with quality service in a timely and friendly manner. Responsibilities vary but may include: cleaning and maintaining the appearance of the public areas of the resort, deep cleaning of assigned areas, setting-up and maintaining complimentary hotel lobby functions including the coffee service and nightly concierge events, cleaning and setting-up meeting room functions, restocking housekeeping stations, delivering service items to guest rooms upon requests from the front desk, and driving shuttle van when needed.

Room Attendant

Room Attendants are responsible for the cleanliness of guest rooms, hallways, and public areas in the hotel. Responsibilities include: servicing guest rooms daily in accordance with hotel procedures, stocking cart with room supplies, and replacing bed linens and replenishing guest room supplies. This position requires strong attention to detail, ability to communicate effectively with guests and team members verbally or in written form, and the ability to bend, lift, and be standing or walking all day.

Maintenance

Chief Maintenance Engineer

The Chief Maintenance Engineer is responsible for maintaining the overall operation of the maintenance department and the appearance and working order of the hotel. The engineer must be able to work independently, as well as, with others. Responsibilities may include: maintaining the exterior of the building, parking lot, and common areas, driving shuttle van as needed, maintaining all equipment in guest rooms, conducting monthly safety inspections and training the staff on safety and emergency procedures, and working with vendors.

Assistant Maintenance Engineer

The Assistant Maintenance Engineer supports the Chief Engineer in maintaining overall appearance and working order of the resort. This position must be able to work independently as well as with others. The Assistant maintenance position requires overall maintenance knowledge and trouble shooting ability with skills in painting, carpentry, equipment, and tool usage.

Grounds

Resort properties with gardens and large outdoor areas employee specialized groundskeepers and landscapers to maintain the exterior of the resort. Most landscapers at resorts are experienced in lawn care and shrub and flower maintenance. Groundskeepers usually maintain the parking lots and walkways as well as the planted areas and are required to be physically fit to push lawnmowers, trim bushes and run leaf blowers. And at most properties, the outside grounds keeping team also maintain the swimming pools.

Concepts

Answer the following questions from the information provided in this unit.

1. What is the difference between the housekeeping and maintenance departments?

2. For which housekeeping and maintenance jobs is physical fitness important? Why?

3. What is the role of the houseperson?

4. How does the housekeeping department contribute to a guests' stay at a resort?

5. Which department services the swimming pools at a resort?

Further Reading

TRAVEL TROUBLESHOOTER

Q My brother, his wife and two kids, ages 17 and 20, recently visited me to attend my wedding. They booked a room for one night at the Best Western Yucca Valley Hotel & Suites. When I returned from my honeymoon, I learned the hotel had tacked on a $250 charge for smoking in a nonsmoking room. My brother and his family do not smoke. Never have. When I called the hotel, I was told that a housekeeper had found ashes on the windowsill in the room. I asked if it was possible if one of the housekeepers or a workman had smoked in the room, not realizing that it was a nonsmoking room. I was told in no uncertain terms that none of the employees had smoked in the room. I asked to speak with the manager and was told she was not there but I could leave my number and she would get back to me. I did this several times over the past two months, but the manager is never there. I've also tried to contact the hotel's owner, but I've never been able to get through to a real person. Can you help?
– Barbara Prestridge, Yucca Valley, Calif.

A Best Western shouldn't have charged a $250 cleaning fee unless it had hard evidence that your brother and his family were lighting up in the room. Finding cigarette ashes on the windowsill may work for the hotel, but not for me. Catching a guest with a cigarette in hand, yes. Cigarette butts in the garbage can? Sure. But ashes on a ledge? I don't know about that.

If a hotel suspects a guest of smoking in a nonsmoking room, there's a right way and a wrong way of handling the situation. The right way is to speak with the guest before checkout, mentioning either the suspicious smell or evidence that someone was puffing away in the room. The wrong way is not to tell anyone about the charges and quietly add them to the final bill.

Am I saying these cleaning charges are bogus? Absolutely not. No one should be smoking in a hotel room, period. The stench of cigarette smoke lingers for many days and seeps into everything, drawing complaints from future guests. I have no sympathy for anyone who smokes in a nonsmoking room, no matter what their circumstances, and I think a $250 fee is letting them off easy. But they may have fined the wrong guest.

One thing about your account raised a red flag: the ages of your brother's children. Had you said they were 7 and 10? It wouldn't have made a difference. But at 17 and 20, you really can't be entirely sure that they aren't sneaking a smoke when mom and dad aren't looking. I'm not saying that happened, only that it makes it a little more difficult to disprove conclusively.

Your communication with Best Western took place entirely by phone, which didn't help your case. I would have sent a short, cordial e-mail to the hotel. It takes a little sleuthing. I couldn't find a Web form to file a complaint, so your best bet would have been to call the property and ask for an email address. That sounds like a lot of trouble, but having a paper trail is important. In the unlikely event you have to take the hotel to small claims court, their responses will become valuable evidence. Also, should you have disputed the $250 charge on your credit card, the correspondence would have been useful. It turns out that was unnecessary. I contacted Best Western on your behalf, and it offered you a $250 voucher, which you accepted.

Practice Makes Perfect

1. Answer the following questions related to the article. Use complete sentences for your answer.

1) How does the author of the response letter feel about smoking in hotel rooms?

2) Who smoked in the hotel room? How do you know?

3) What was the resolution to the dispute between Best Western and Barbara Prestridge?

4) What evidence did Best Western have of someone smoking in the hotel room?

5) What suggestions and advice does the author of the response letter have for people who have a dispute with a hotel or resort?

2. Match the following words from the previous article to the definition that best matches. Draw a line to connect the matching pairs.

1) Evidence •	• A) The ridge of a window
2) Paper trail •	• B) Proof
3) Ledge •	• C) To say
4) Conclusively •	• D) Physical evidence of communication
5) Light up •	• E) Pity
6) Windowsill •	• F) Shelf or ridge
7) Mention •	• G) Looking for information, perhaps secretly
8) Sympathy •	• H) Irrevocably
9) Sleuthing •	• I) Coupon or gift certificate
10) Voucher •	• J) To smoke

3. Use the following word in a sentence.

1) Light up: ______________________________

2) Windowsill: ______________________________

3) Mention: ______________________________

Just Do It

Verbs are the parts of speech that indicate action. Phrasal verbs are two-word verbs, prepositional verbs or two verbs used together. Review the two phrasal verbs below.

To get worked up

- To easily become emotionally upset about something

EXAMPLE:

- When it comes to my job, I easily get worked up.

To hand something over

- To give something to someone, to relinquish something to someone.

EXAMPLE:

- John finally handed the wallet over to the police.

UNIT 5

The Squeaky Wheel Gets the Grease

Unit Goals

- Build vocabulary and conversation skills for managing resort guests
- Practice practical resort-specific English
- Learn about jobs associated with guest relations and management
- Develop reading comprehension skills with career-relevant articles

Vocabulary

- Earplugs
- To resolve
- To stomach a thought
- On the house
- To come right up
- Willingness
- To treat someone
- Ordeal
- To malfunction / a malfunction
- To lose one's mind
- Obnoxious
- Unflattering
- Carping
- Disinclined
- Tendency
- Discretion
- Spoiled
- To gripe
- Notoriously
- Intuitive

Let's Get Started

Translate these common questions relating to guest complaints at a resort. Resort staff would ask some questions, and guests would ask others. In the blank provided, write the letter "S" for staff or the letter "G" for guest, indicating who would ask the question.

1. Do you offer room service? ____

2. When would you like to pick up your laundry? ____

3. Can you please fix the leaky faucet? ____

4. Can I provide you with additional toiletries? ____

5. Can you please bring me two more towels? ____

6. Can you leave dirty towels on the floor? ____

7. Can you clean my room every two days, please? ____

8. Is the air conditioner working yet? ____

9. Is that loud noise from room construction? ____

10. Can you please put tissue in the bathroom in the lobby? ____

Conversation I

Seung Jae: Reception. How may I help you?

Dawn: Hi. This is Ms. Marie, in room 1004.

Seung Jae: What can I do for you tonight?

Dawn: As you know, it is 2:00 in the morning. I am tired. I have a conference tomorrow and I can't sleep. You put me in a room next to the elevator and all I can hear is other guests entering and exiting the elevator.

Seung Jae: Ms. Marie, did you indicate that you did not want this room?

Dawn: What difference does it make? Who wants a room where they cannot sleep?

Seung Jae: Yes, I understand. I can have earplugs brought to you immediately and we can move your room in the morning. Would you like that?

Dawn: Yes, that will be fine, but what I really would have liked is a quiet room from the start.

Seung Jae: Yes, Ms. Marie. I understand. I will let the daytime employees know to move you when they arrive. Again, my sincere apologies.

Dawn: Very well. Good night.

Conversation II

Seung Jae: How was your meal tonight?

Dawn: Actually, now that you ask, it wasn't very good. I am a bit disappointed.

Seung Jae: What was the problem? Perhaps I can resolve it for you.

Dawn: Well, I wasn't going to say anything, but I found a hair in my salad. I pulled it out, but you should understand that is not appetizing.

Seung Jae: No, it's not. Can I bring you another salad?

Dawn: No, that's ok. I can't stomach the thought of another salad. Thanks, though.

Seung Jae: What would you like me to do? I feel terrible.

Dawn: Please remove the salad from my bill. I should not be expected to pay for food I didn't eat because it was dirty.

Seung Jae: Most certainly. I will have that taken off of your bill. Can I bring you a dessert, on the house?

Dawn: Well, that might be nice. I have never met a dessert I didn't like.

Seung Jae: Excellent. Chocolate cake, coming right up.

Conversation III

Seung Jae: Good afternoon. Are you enjoying this beautiful weather we're having?

Dawn: Yes, but it would be nice if I could use the pool.

Seung Jae: Which pool? Is there a pool out of service?

Dawn: Well, it should be. It's filthy. You should not expect resort guests to swim in a dirty pool.

Seung Jae: Which pool is this?

Dawn: The Lanai Pool, near Lulu's Grill.

Seung Jae: I appreciate you telling me. I will phone maintenance right away. I can have it cleaned in 60 minutes.

Dawn: Fine. I appreciate your willingness to listen. I guess I just expected more.

Seung Jae: You have the right to expect more, Ms. Marie. This is a world-class resort. Here, you should get the best.

Dawn: Then I look forward to a good swim, right after lunch.

Seung Jae: Let me make a call and have your lunch taken care of for you. It would be my pleasure to treat you today; after all you have been through an ordeal in order to swim.

Conversation IV

Seung Jae: Will you be checking in today?

Dawn: Yes, I have a reservation under the name Marie. It's a single room with an ocean view.

Seung Jae: Just one moment while I check out system. (He checks the computer.) Oh, unfortunately, we do not have a reservation in our system for you.

Dawn: What? What did you say? You don't have my reservation? That is impossible! I made that reservation weeks ago. Check again!

Seung Jae: Perhaps you made the reservation with a different resort. I am sorry, Ms. Marie, but now we are full for the evening.

Dawn: You had better find room for me. I did my job and reserved a room. Now, do your job and get it for me. This is your fault, not mine and I want you to fix it!

Seung Jae: I cannot evict another guest, Ms. Marie. Let me find the Operations Manager for you. He might be able to find a solution for you today.

Mr. Scott: Ms. Marie, I would ask you how you are, but I think I already know. Now, let me look at your ID and see if I can find the root of this problem. (He checks the computer.) Yes. Here it is. Our system lost many reservations, including yours.

Dawn: Thank god there is proof of my reservation. I felt like I was losing my mind. Now, tell me, how can we fix this?

A Job Well Done

Review the 9 most common guest complaints about each resort department below. Brainstorm with a partner how a resort can avoid these complaints.

Front Desk Operations

Unhelpful Staff

There is nothing worse than encountering a mean or nasty receptionist. Perhaps they are unhappy because they missed a raise in pay or recently ended a relationship. Whatever the reason is, it doesn't matter. The guest should never have to suffer. Unhelpful or mean employees have the power to make the guest very unhappy, very quickly.

Inaccurate Star Rating

The problem in London, for example, is that there is no single regulatory body which controls star ratings. It is therefore possible, in fact probable, that many resorts and hotels decide themselves what star rating to be.

No Booking on Arrival

99% of resorts and hotels tend to overbook every night on the basis that someone will cancel at the last minute. When this happens not only do they charge a cancellation fee but they have probably had an instant taker for the room so the revenue is suddenly increased. Resorts differ on their policies.

Overcharged

It's surprising how many travelers do not check their itemized bill when checking out. Extras such as a paid movie or a short from the minibar can go on the wrong room bill easily.

A Room Next to an Elevator

Resort guest desire a good night's sleep. This may mean sensitive guests, or guests with small children may not be suitable for rooms near elevators. After all, nobody wants to hear other guests coming and going all night long.

Housekeeping and Maintenance

Bed Bugs

This is a very serious complaint and one that the management dreads. These horrid creatures can be found in carpets, woodwork, beds and travelers luggage. They can last up to one year without blood as food. Check out the sheets for small specks of blood. You can also pull back the bed sheets and check the mattress seams and bedside drawers for signs such as the bug itself or minute small black droppings or dried blood. If a guest complains of bedbugs there is no way to win; bedbugs are bad.

Dirty Resort Grounds

Guests have higher standards for resorts than they do their own homes. Guests come from all over the world to enjoy a relaxing vacation and will notice an unkempt resort. This is true for the guest rooms, lobby area, leisure facilities such as the pool and sauna.

Food Services

Substandard Restaurant

No guest wants to eat poor quality food, especially on vacation. All guests, especially North American and European guests, expect the same quality and service they get in their home countries. Bad food, dirty restaurants and unfriendly staff draw many complaints.

Poor Room Service

Room service is expensive. When a guest orders in, the food quality and service should match that of the restaurant. When it doesn't, there is room for a complaint. Americans might complain first about service and then about food, while French guests will complain about food quality first. The nature of the complaint will depend on the nationality of the guest, but no guest wants poor service or bad food.

Concepts

Answer the following questions from the information provided in this unit.

1. What are the top complaints for housekeeping? Why do you think resort guests complain about these things?

2. Why does Seung Jae give Ms. Marie a free lunch?

3. How did the resort fix the problem with low food quality? Was this a good solution? Would you have been satisfied?

4. Why did Ms. Marie complain about the pool? Does a guest have a right to complain about facilities?

5. Why did the resort offer to bring earplugs to Ms. Marie's room? Why didn't they simply move her room when she called to complain?

Further Reading

Who Are the Most Obnoxious Tourists?

According to a recent international survey, the French are now considered the most obnoxious tourists from European nations, behind only Indians and the last-place Chinese as the worst among countries worldwide. And it's not just the rest of the world that has a gripe with the Gallic attitude: the French also finished second to last among nations ranking the popularity of their own tourists who vacation at home.

But it's the unflattering image being reflected from abroad that may give pause to the millions of French travelers now heading off to summer-vacation destinations across the globe. Will this move them to improve behavior the poll characterized as impolite, prone to loud carping and inattentive to local customs? If so, that's just the start: the study also describes the voyageur François as often unwilling or unable to communicate in foreign languages, and particularly disinclined to spend money when they don't have to. Overall, French travelers landed 19th out of 21 nations worldwide, far behind the first-place Japanese, considered the most polite, quiet and tidy. Following the Japanese, as most-liked tourists, were the Germans, British and Canadians. Americans finished in 11th place alongside the Thais.

The survey was taken by employees in 4,000 hotels in Germany, the U.K., Italy, France, Canada and the U.S. for the French travel website Expedia.fr. The study asked respondents to rank clients by nationality on criteria of general attitude, politeness, tendency to complain, willingness to speak local languages, interest in sampling local cuisine, readiness to spend money, generosity, cleanliness, discretion and elegance. Many replies simply conformed to long-established reputations: Italians, for example, were described as the best-dressed tourists, with the French not far behind.

American tourists fared well in some surprising ways. Despite being notoriously language-limited, for example, they top the list of tourists credited with trying to speak local languages the most, with the French, Chinese, Japanese, Italians and Russians coming in last in the local-language rankings. Does this mean Americans are the most polyglot tourists on the planet? Maybe not, says Expedia's marketing director for Europe, Timothée de Roux, who says the poll's focus on hotel operators may explain the counterintuitive outcome.

De Roux says external factors similarly account for why Americans wound up as the biggest-spending and best-tipping tourists, while Germans and the French were among the worst penny-pinchers. "Our findings show the average French employee will get 37 vacation days spread over seven trips in 2008, versus 14 for an American - who won't even take them all," de Roux says. "That means the French tourist will more tightly budget his or her spending over more trips, while the American spends freely on the one or two vacations taken all year."

By contrast, the poll finds that the French and Americans are similar in being perceived as critical and rude when they travel - though for different reasons. "When they go abroad, French travelers demand the same quality they'd get at home," de Roux says. "Americans, by contrast, demand the same exceptional service they are used to at home, which is why they rank as the loudest, most inclined to complain and among the least polite."

Practice Makes Perfect

Reading Comprehension

1. Answer the following questions related to the article. Use complete sentences for your answer.

1) Why do the French spend less on vacations than Americans?

2) Who are the worst European tourists? Why? Who are the worst tourists in the world? Why?

3) How do you think Koreans rank among global tourists? Why?

4) Why are Americans likely to complain while on vacation in another country?

5) How were respondents asked to reply? How were countries graded?

2. Match the following words from the previous article to the definition that best matches. Draw a line to connect the matching pairs.

1) Obnoxious •	• A) By instinct
2) Unflattering •	• B) Infamously
3) Carping •	• C) Flawed
4) Disinclined •	• D) Tact
5) Tendency •	• E) Complain
6) Discretion •	• F) Inclination
7) Spoiled •	• G) Intolerable
8) Gripe •	• H) Ugly
9) Notoriously •	• I) Complaining
10) Intuitively •	• J) Reluctant

3. Use the following word in a sentence.

1) Gripe: ______________________________

2) Carping: ______________________________

3) Obnoxious: ______________________________

Just Do It

Verbs are the parts of speech that indicate action. Phrasal verbs are two-word verbs, prepositional verbs or two verbs used together. Review the two phrasal verbs below.

To touch something up

- To fix minor flaws in something

EXAMPLE:

- When I finished with the paint in the hall, I touched up the lobby.

To blow someone or something off

- To skip a meeting or an event

EXAMPLE:

- John blew off the meeting to spend time with his girlfriend.

UNIT 6 Shop Till You Drop

Unit Goals

- Build vocabulary and conversation skills for resort shopping
- Practice practical resort-specific English
- Learn about jobs associated with resort shopping and retail outlets
- Develop reading comprehension skills with career-relevant articles

Vocabulary

- Boutique
- To reach
- To tend to do
- Souvenirs
- Tacky
- Payments
- Receipt
- Fixed
- Circumstances
- Arcade
- To deem
- Limited
- To swap
- Curt
- To stare
- To jeer
- To range from (A) to (B)
- Chains
- Chic
- To reproduce

Let's Get Started

Translate these common questions relating to resort shopping. Resort staff would ask some questions, and guests would ask others. In the blank provided, write the letter "S" for staff or the letter "G" for guest, indicating who would ask the question.

1. Do you have a bigger size in this same shirt? ____

2. Would you like the receipt with you or in the bag? ____

3. Does this come in another color? ____

4. Where do I sign? ____

5. Can you meet me at the register? ____

6. Do you accept traveler's checks? ____

7. Will that be cash or credit? ____

8. Can I get a discount? ____

9. Would you like this gift wrapped today? ____

10. Have you been to our other location yet? ____

Conversation I

Seung Jae: Welcome to Lake House Boutique. How may I assist you?

Dawn: Hello. I'm just looking around for now, thanks.

Seung Jae: Take your time and be sure to check out our new resort wear clothing line.

Dawn: Thanks, I'll be sure to do that. (She browses the store.) Sir, can you please reach this blouse for me? It's the one on the highest rack. I can't reach it.

Seung Jae: The white one with lace? Which size would you like?

Dawn: Is it Asian or Western sized?

Seung Jae: This is measured in Western sizes.

Dawn: Then I would like a size small, please.

Seung Jae: Great. Can I show you the blue one, too? I think it would look great on you.

Dawn: Sure. I'll try both. Can you bring me one in a small and the other in a medium?

Conversation II

Seung Jae: Did you find what you were looking for today?

Dawn: I found more than I was looking for.

Seung Jae: That tends to happen here. There are a lot of unique gifts here.

Dawn: I agree. I have not seen souvenirs like these before.

Seung Jae: That is because they are handmade by a local artist. The resort tries to support the local economy and talent.

Dawn: That is fantastic. I will take two, then.

Seung Jae: Would you like gift boxes today?

Dawn: Yes, please remove the price from the items. Leaving the price tag on a gift is so tacky.

Seung Jae: I agree. Your total today is $145.75. Would you like to use cash or a card today?

Dawn: I will use my Samsung card today. Can I put that on two payments?

Seung Jae: Unfortunately, we do not offer that service. If you call your card provider when you get home you can arrange multiple payments.

Dawn: Great. Here is my card. Where do I sign?

Seung Jae: Sign here, please. Would you like your receipt with you or in the bag?

Conversation III

Dawn: Hi, I have a question. Can you help me?

Seung Jae: Sure. What's your question?

Dawn: I would like to buy this candle and I think it is the last one, but it's damaged. I think it was the sample.

Seung Jae: Let me check the inventory to see if we have another. (He checks the computer.) Yes, it looks like you are right; that is the last one.

Dawn: I thought so. Well, I think I want it, but I don't want to pay full price for a damaged item. Can you give me a discount?

Seung Jae: Our prices are normally fixed, but given the circumstances, I can offer you 10% off the candle.

Dawn: I'm sorry but 10% just isn't enough. It's the sample, but it's also damaged. Would you be willing to give me 20% off?

Seung Jae: I can give you 20% off, but the item will then be nonrefundable. Is that okay?

Dawn: Sure, that's great. I really love the scent of the candle, so I know I won't return it.

Seung Jae: Perfect. Let me wrap this up for you. Can you meet me at the register?

Dawn: Sure. Also, do you accept traveler's checks?

Seung Jae: No, unfortunately, we don't, but we accept US dollars, local currency and all major credit cards.

Conversation IV

Seung Jae: Ms. Marie, any plans for the day?

Dawn: Well, I wanted to pick up a couple of gifts to take back home for my friends. Any suggestions for where I should go?

Seung Jae: Well, the resort has a beautiful shopping arcade. You should start there.

Dawn: Really? I haven't seen it yet. Which shops are there?

Seung Jae: We have excellent clothing and accessory boutiques, as well as stores specializing in a variety of sports, like golf and scuba diving.

Dawn: Wow, that sounds great. I was hoping to buy some tea or coffee to take home. I want something nicely presented.

Seung Jae: Yes, Ms. Marie, presentation counts. In this case, I suggest Tea Time, on the 3rd floor of the arcade. It has amazing teas that are boxes and wrapped. The boxes, paper wrapping and tea are all locally produced.

Mr. Scott: That is just the kind of gift I was looking for. Thanks, I will start there and work my way around the arcade.

Dawn: Take my card, and call this desk if you have any special shopping or ordering needs. I will do my best to help you get what you need before your departure.

A Job Well Done

Review the job descriptions below for resort shopping and retail personnel.

Retail Store Manager

The main responsibility of a retail manager is handling and overseeing all the day-to-day processes that are carried out in the store. The manager controls the product inventory, salespersons, goods for display, sales, etc. The manager will also take care of the interests of the members in his sales team, as they are the ones who are in direct contact with the consumers.

Retail Sales Associate

A sales associate is expected to generate sales by providing outstanding customer service. Every customer needs to feel welcome to shop at the resort. Greeting the customer, attending to his needs and building a loyal customer base are some of the duties of a retail sales associate. The sales associate is expected to know about promotional offers and encourage the customer to buy the products promoted by the store. The associate is also expected to be aware of the merchandise available in the shop and arrange for items not available on the floor of the store. The exact nature of the job would depend on the kind of store that employs the retail sales associate. In addition to assisting customers and generating sales, the job description of retail sales associate includes making out sales checks; receiving cash, checks, debit and credit card payments; bagging purchases and giving receipts. They may be required to open and close cash registers and may be held responsible for the contents of their register.

Concepts

Answer the following questions from the information provided in this unit.

1. What are the responsibilities of a retail sales associate?

2. What is a shopping arcade? What shops might typically be in an arcade?

3. Why would a resort have a golf shop or a scuba diving shop in their arcade?

4. What does a retail manager do? How is this different from an associate?

5. Why does Ms. Marie want the price tag removed from the item she is buying?

Further Reading

Asia's 'Big' Shopping Problem

Even though countries like China are "getting bigger", being plus-sized can be particularly demoralizing in Asia's cosmopolitan cities, where weight-watching is practically a national pastime. "You switch on the TV in Singapore and it's all about slimming programs, slim is good, slim is beautiful," says Erica Sim, 30, owner of shopping portal Big n Beautiful. She has dreadful memories of Singapore's Trim and Fit (TAF) program, which forced diets and exercise on students deemed overweight. "It was so embarrassing to be skipping rope in front of my friends who were enjoying their break-time snack." Erica laments the limited clothing options for larger Asian women. "If it's available, it's at a non-affordable price. If it's affordable, the design is ugly; very aunty-ish." To make matters worse, some shop assistants are downright cruel to customers. "We have swapped and shared horror stories of curvy ladies entering boutiques and being turned away with a curt comment, or getting unfriendly stares and jeers," write Candy Chow, Daphne Aw and Wendy Chow of Big On Attitude, a Singapore-based web shop for "bold, beautiful wear."

Quite a few foreigners, who are not considered large in their home countries, suddenly run into difficulties when buying clothes. Owen Rosa, 33, is a business developer who has lived in Japan for over ten years. At 6 foot 1 (183 centimeters) and a muscular 200 pounds (93 kg), he's given up on visiting local shops. "Sometimes, the clerks will ask me to try something on, but most of the time I can't even put it on all the way. It would always create a feeling that foreigners are not wanted in Japan."

The good news: Asia has a growing number of choices for large and tall shoppers -- as well as communities that celebrate plus-sized beauty.

Global Clothing Retailers

Asian designs tend to be sized smaller to fit the regional market. But global brands cater to global customers, meaning you can find size US 14 (UK 16) or higher on the rack. Try shopping at Next, Topshop, Gap, Dorothy Perkins and Marks & Spencer. Asia-based retail chains offer a greater range of sizes. These include Hong Kong's Bossini and Giordano, Singapore's Sant Rolane and York Boutique, and Japan's Uniqlo.

Department Stores

Most department stores have a selection for taller and larger customers. The section is typically called Plus or Queen; in Japan's Marui it's known as Model. However, the fit may not be larger than a US 10 or 12.

Online Stores and Communities

Plus-sized web communities have sprung up to provide clothes and solidarity. Singapore's Big n Beautiful and Big On Attitude source chic clothes made for curves, many of which are locally made and inexpensive. Taiwan's Color Pencil features photos of big girls looking gorgeous in street style coordinates.

Custom-tailored Fashion

There's no better place than Asia to get custom-made clothes for reasonable prices. Bring a picture of a runway piece and your local tailor can reproduce it in any size and material. You can also place orders online: China's Fanplusfriend custom-fits Gothic Lolita, cosplay and Harajuku styles that would otherwise only come in "free size" (about a US $4).

Practice Makes Perfect

Reading Comprehension

1. Answer the following questions related to the article. Use complete sentences for your answer.

1) What does the title of this article suggest? What is the problem?

2) What problems do bigger Asian women have when buying clothes? What do they encounter when they shop?

3) What is the good news offered by this article?

4) How does Owen Rosa, a man, feel about shopping in Japan?

5) Which global clothing brands are suggested for larger Asian people? Which of these brands are available in Korea?

2. Match the following words from the previous article to the definition that best matches. Draw a line to connect the matching pairs.

1) To deem •	• A) Replicate
2) Limited •	• B) Stylish
3) To swap •	• C) Many locations
4) Curt •	• D) Assortment
5) To stare •	• E) To laugh at
6) To jeer •	• F) To watch continuously
7) Range •	• G) Rude
8) Chains •	• H) To exchange
9) Chic •	• I) Inadequate
10) To reproduce •	• J) To think or believe

3. Use the following word in a sentence.

1) To stare: ____________________

2) Limited: ____________________

3) Chic: ____________________

Just Do It

Verbs are the parts of speech that indicate action. Phrasal verbs are two-word verbs, prepositional verbs or two verbs used together. Review the two phrasal verbs below.

To buy something up

- To buy all of something, the entire supply

EXAMPLE:

- I love this lotion so much that I bought it all up.

To buy something back

- To buy something from someone whom you have previously sold it to

EXAMPLE:

- Can I buy it back? I decided I actually need it.

CHAPTER

II

Resort Sports

UNIT 1

Pool Party

Unit Goals

- Build vocabulary and conversation skills for resort sports
- Practice practical resort-specific English
- Learn about the gear and accessories necessary for waterparks and pool areas
- Profile waterparks and pool areas
- Profile Hawaii, US, Hawaiian cuisine and culture

Vocabulary

- Breeze
- Rarely
- Windward
- Leeward
- Shelter
- Topping
- Roasted
- Pit
- Patty
- To perpetuate
- Righteous
- Environment
- Bodyboarding
- To take a dip
- To improve
- Inflatable
- Raft
- Cabana
- Facility
- To be eager

Let's Get Started

Translate these common questions relating to waterparks. Resort staff would ask some questions, and guests would ask others. In the blank provided, write the letter "S" for staff or the letter "G" for guest, indicating who would ask the question.

1. Do you have a swimming cap? ____

2. Is there a wave pool here? ____

3. Will you rent a locker today? ____

4. Where is the locker room? ____

5. Is there an 'adults only' area? ____

6. Would you like a map of the park? ____

7. Can I get an extra towel? ____

8. Where is the snack bar? ____

9. Is there a discount for foreigners? ____

10. What time does the park close today? ____

Conversation I

Seung Jae: You look like you are ready for the pool.

Dawn: I sure am. All of this golfing, diving and shopping has me exhausted. I am totally ready for a lazy day.

Seung Jae: Sounds relaxing. Will you be heading to the waterpark?

Dawn: Yes, I am. I was going to take the shuttle bus over there now.

Seung Jae: Good idea. It's possible to walk, but in this heat, it might be tiring.

Dawn: I agree. I can't wait to jump in. I love floating around the lazy river on a tube.

Seung Jae: You're not a fan of the waterslides?

Dawn: Sometimes I like the thrill, but not today. I might get into the wave pool though.

Seung Jae: I see. To be honest, I really prefer a regular swimming pool.

Dawn: Does the waterpark have one of those?

Seung Jae: Yes, actually, it has three.

Dawn: Great. All this talk of waterparks has me eager. I'll see you later.

Conversation II

Seung Jae: Welcome to Bear Mountain Waterpark. Is this your first visit?

Dawn: Yes, it is.

Seung Jae: Then I would like to tell you about the rules. First, a swimming cap is required while enjoying any water facility. Also, no running inside the park is permitted. We ask that you secure your valuables in a locker, as we are not responsible for lost or stolen items. Do you have any questions?

Dawn: Yes, do you rent tubes? I would like one, but I don't want to buy it.

Seung Jae: Yes. We have a rental services counter. You can rent towels, lockers, tubes and cabanas.

Dawn: What is a cabana?

Seung Jae: Around the various facilities, we have simple shelters. They are hut-like houses, which shelter our guests from the hot sun. It's the perfect place to relax.

Dawn: Wow, that sounds perfect. How much is a cabana?

Seung Jae: Cabanas are $20 for the entire day. It's a good value, if you ask me.

Dawn: It looks like I need a tube and a cabana.

Conversation III

Dawn: Excuse me, sir, I think I have lost my child.

Seung Jae: Okay, please stay calm and we will find your child.

Dawn: Her name is Charlotte. She is 6 years old.

Seung Jae: Can you describe what she is wearing today?

Dawn: She is wearing a bright pink one-piece bathing suit, and has a white swim cap on. She has blonde hair and blue eyes.

Seung Jae: Very good. Where did you see her last?

Dawn: We were standing next to the children's wading pool.

Seung Jae: And when was that?

Dawn: It was 8 minutes ago.

Seung Jae: Let me radio this to all the waterpark employees. We will lock-down the park until she is found; nobody can leave until she is found.

Conversation IV

Seung Jae: How was the waterpark, Ms. Marie?

Dawn: It was fantastic. I rented a cabana, dipped in the pool and even went bodyboarding.

Seung Jae: That sure sounds like a full day.

Dawn: It was a good day. I am glad I went.

Seung Jae: Did you try the water slides?

Dawn: I didn't try the slide, but I did try the raft run.

Seung Jae: That must be new. What is it?

Dawn: It's like a water slide, only wider. You ride down the slide in an inflatable raft and land in a big swimming pool.

Seung Jae: Sounds like Bear Mountain has made some improvements. I may have to visit again.

Well Played

Resort guests sometimes vacation in order to relax and participate in recreational activities. Review the following information about resort sports.

Waterparks

For families with children, or the child within the adult resort guest, a waterpark offers visitors escape from the hot sun, or an indoor spa-like holiday. Waterparks draw millions of visitors each year, and are becoming big business in the resort world. A waterpark is an amusement park that features waterplay areas, such as water slides, splash pads, spraygrounds (water playgrounds), lazy rivers, or other recreational bathing, swimming, and barefooting environments. Waterparks may also have some type of artificial surfing or bodyboarding environment, such as a wave pool.

Waterparks have grown in popularity since their introduction in the late 1940s. The United States has the largest and most concentrated waterpark market, with over a thousand waterparks and dozens of new parks opening each year. With 5 indoor waterparks, Wisconsin Dells, Wisconsin, is recognized as the "Waterpark Capital of the World."

Waterparks emerging from spas continue to more closely resemble mountain resorts as they become four-season destinations.

The first ever indoor waterpark was built in Edmonton, Alberta, Canada in 1985. It also includes one of the world's largest indoor wave pool, waterslides of varying degrees, tube rides, zip lines, bungee jumping, and hot tubs.

Concepts

Answer the following questions from the information provided in this unit.

1. What is a waterpark? How is it different from an amusement park?

2. Where was the first indoor waterpark?

3. What can a resort guest expect to find at a waterpark?

4. Which country has the most waterparks? How many new parks open each year?

5. What is Wisconsin Dells famous for? Why?

Going Places

Culture and Geography

Read the following information about Hawaii, Hawaiian culture, climate and cuisine.

Focus on Hawaii, United States of America

Hawaii, US

Population: 1,288,198 (2009 estimate)

Capital and Largest City: Honolulu

Languages: English, Hawaiian

Motto: The Life of the Land is Perpetuated in Righteousness

Number of islands: 8

Claim to fame: The birthplace of US President Barack Obama

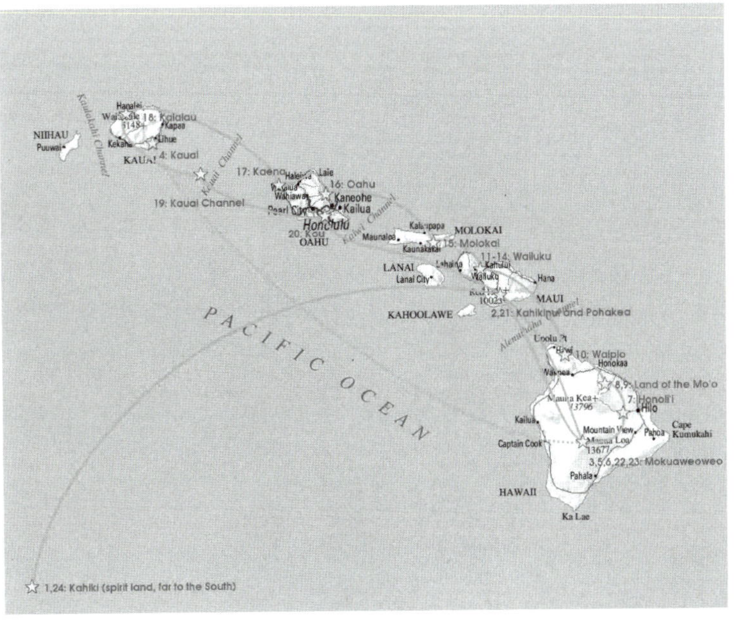

Cuisine

Modern cuisine of Hawaii is a fusion of many cuisines brought by multiethnic immigrants to the Hawaiian Islands. American, Chinese, Filipino, Japanese, Korean, Polynesian and Portuguese influences are found in Hawaiian foods. Many local restaurants serve 'plate lunch' featuring two scoops of rice, a simplified version of American macaroni salad, and a variety of different toppings ranging from a hamburger patty, a fried egg, and gravy of a Loco Moco, Japanese style tonkatsu or the traditional lu'au favorite, kalua pig. Kalua pig is a whole pig that is slow roasted in an underground barbeque pit for many hours. Loco Moco is a dish that was created at the Lincoln Grill in Hilo, Hawaii in 1949.

Climate

Hawaii's climate is tropical, but breezes keep the islands cool and comfortable. Summer highs are usually in the upper 80s °F, (around 31 °C) during the day and mid 70s, (around 24 °C) at night. Winter day temperatures are usually in the low to mid 80s, (around 28 °C) and (at low elevation) seldom dipping below the mid 60s (18 °C) at night. Snow, not usually associated with tropics, falls at 4,205 meters (13,796 ft) on Mauna Kea and Mauna Loa on the Big Island in some winter months. Snow rarely falls on Haleakala. Mount Waialeale, on Kauai, has the second highest average annual rainfall on Earth, about 460 inches (11.7 m). Most of Hawaii has only two seasons: the dry season from May to October, and the wet season from October to April. Local climates vary considerably on each island, based upon location relative to the higher mountains. Windward environments are very cloudy. Because of this, most Hawaiian resorts are on the sunny leeward side of mountain ranges.

Practice Makes Perfect

1. Answer the following questions related to this section. Use complete sentences for your answer.

1) What is Loco Moco? How was it invented?

2) What happens on Mauna Kea and Mauna Loa? Why is this surprising?

3) Which nations influence modern Hawaiian cuisine? What do you expect Hawaiian food to taste like?

4) What is a plate lunch?

5) What are the seasons like in Hawaii? What are the seasonal high and low temperatures?

2. Match the following words from the previous section to the definition that best matches. Draw a line to connect the matching pairs.

1) Breeze	A) Almost never
2) Rarely	B) Upwind from the point of reference
3) Windward	C) Seasoning added to a dish, on the top
4) Leeward	D) Honorable
5) Topping	E) Light wind
6) Roasted	F) Hole in the ground
7) Pit	G) Meadow
8) Patty	H) Continue
9) Perpetuate	I) Round, flat piece of meat, usually hamburger
10) Righteous	J) Downwind from the point of reference

3. Use the following word in a sentence.

1) Roasted: ____________________

2) Breeze: ____________________

3) Patty: ____________________

Just Do It

Verbs are the parts of speech that indicate action. Phrasal verbs are two-word verbs, prepositional verbs or two verbs used together. Review the two phrasal verbs below.

To ask around about something

- To ask many people about the same thing

EXAMPLE:

- I asked around about the bus schedule.

To break something in

- To wear something or use something a few times so it doesn't look or feel new

EXAMPLE:

- Last week, I broke my running shoes in.

UNIT 2 Bunny Slopes

Unit Goals

- Build vocabulary and conversation skills for resort sports
- Practice practical resort-specific English
- Learn about the gear and accessories necessary for resort winter sports
- Profile winter sports
- Profile Switzerland, Swiss cuisine and culture

Vocabulary

- Gondola
- Ski lift
- To zip down something
- Ski bibs / ski jacket and pants
- Mittens / gloves
- Ski boots
- Ski bindings
- Bunny hill (ski terminology)
- Black diamond (ski terminology)
- Poles (ski gear)
- Freshwater
- Plateau
- Glacier
- Consumer
- Vineyard
- Ancient
- Pasture
- Graze
- Populous
- Temperate

Let's Get Started

Translate these common questions relating to winter sports. Resort staff would ask some questions, and guests would ask others. In the blank provided, write the letter "S" for staff or the letter "G" for guest, indicating who would ask the question.

1. Do you ski or snowboard? ____

2. How is the snow today? ____

3. Will you rent skis? ____

4. Where is the beginner slope? ____

5. Does the gondola lift cost more? ____

6. How many days will you ski with us? ____

7. Would you like a ski-in, ski-out room? ____

8. Why is the expert slope closed? ____

9. Would you like to purchase a night lift ticket? ____

10. Will there be a discount for using a specific credit card? ____

Conversation I

Seung Jae: Are you here to ski, or snowboard?

Dawn: I am a skier. I can't imagine flying down the mountain on a snowboard.

Seung Jae: I think that is the beauty of winter sports; there is something for everyone.

Dawn: I would have to agree. But I really enjoy skiing. Nothing feels the same as the wind on my face as I zip down the mountain.

Seung Jae: You're in luck. We have fresh powder today; none of the artificial snow.

Dawn: That's fantastic. I prefer the real stuff. It's softer than machine-made snow.

Seung Jae: Yes, but not every country is as blessed as we are. We have world-class ski conditions.

Dawn: Yes, you do. Do you also have a ski shop where I could replace my goggles?

Seung Jae: Of course. In the shopping arcade, as you walk toward the ski lifts, you'll find the ski shop.

Dawn: Thanks, I am quite eager to hit the slopes.

Conversation II

Seung Jae: How were the bunny hills today?

Dawn: Bunny hills? Those are for beginners. I did one run on the beginners slope and upgraded.

Seung Jae: So, you went to the black diamond runs?

Dawn: Are you serious? I am not an expert either. I am an intermediate skier. I don't want to fall down the mountain; I want to ski down the mountain.

Seung Jae: I suppose there is a fundamental difference between falling and skiing.

Dawn: And that is why I ski instead of snowboard. I tried it once and spent all day on my backside.

Seung Jae: I heard it's difficult to learn, but easier to master than skiing. Why not give it another try?

Dawn: I'm not sure I have the courage. Frankly, it was a painful experience.

Seung Jae: It's worth another shot. You can use the same lift ticket for skiing and snowboarding. What do you have to lose?

Dawn: Oh, just my dignity, but I suppose you're right.

Conversation III

Dawn: I will need a rental today.

Seung Jae: Ski or board?

Dawn: I'll rent skis today. Actually, for the week, please.

Seung Jae: What is your boot size?

Dawn: I'm not sure. My regular shoe size is 245, or a $7\frac{1}{2}$ American. Does that help?

Seung Jae: Let's try a size 8, then. You'll need some extra room for your ski socks.

Dawn: I guess you're right. Also, I would like a junior ski. I am quite short, and regular adult skis are a little too long for me.

Seung Jae: Very well, Ms. Marie. Will you need poles?

Dawn: Yes, please. I also would like to buy a new hat. Can I get that here?

Seung Jae: You can buy gear at the ski shop. It's just around the corner.

Conversation IV

Seung Jae: How was your day on the mountain?

Dawn: Well, it was interesting.

Seung Jae: Interesting? Is that good or bad?

Dawn: It was a bit of both, actually. I had a fantastic day skiing, but I accidentally went out-of-bounds and off the marked trail. I was lost for about 2 hours.

Seung Jae: Oh my God! That can be really dangerous. Are you okay?

Dawn: I'm fine now, but there was a point in time where I was scared. I decided to stay calm, and just make my way down, slowly.

Seung Jae: We try to mark the trails clearly here at the resort, but there are places that are a little remote, that might have been overlooked.

Dawn: I was on the trail, and the next thing I knew, there was no more groomed snow. I was skiing in the wild of the forest.

Seung Jae: Can you recall where you were? Maybe I can send ski patrol up to that area to re-mark the course.

Dawn: I was near the Rainbow Trail, on the west side of the mountain.

Seung Jae: I'll send someone there today. Take care, Ms. Marie, and be careful.

Dawn: Of course, and thank you for your concern. I'll be sure to ski on the tail tomorrow.

Well Played

Resort guests sometimes vacation in order to relax and participate in recreational activities. Review the following information about resort sports.

Winter Sports

It can't be hot and sunny everywhere, and it can't be summer all year long. Some resort guests take their holiday in the mountains, escaping sounds of the city and craving fresh alpine air. For the adventurous, winter sports provide the necessary adrenalin rush.

Skiing is a recreational activity that uses skis for traveling over snow. Skis are used with boots that connect to the ski with use of a binding. Skiing can be grouped into two general categories. The older of the two disciplines originated in Scandinavia, uses bindings that attach at the toes of the skier's boots, but not at the heels. This is commonly called Nordic skiing. Alpine skiing, more often called "downhill skiing", originated in the European Alps, and is characterized by bindings that attach at both the toe and the heel of the skier's boot. Downhill skiing can take place on a pre-set course, or free-style on the snowy slope of a forested mountain.

Snowboarding is a sport that involves going down a slope on a board attached to a rider's feet, using a special boot set onto mounted binding. The development of snowboarding was inspired by skateboarding, surfing and skiing. It was developed in the US in the 1960s and 70s. Snowboarding became a Winter Olympic Sport in 1998. Snowboarding was developed to perform jumps and flips, called tricks.

Fashion and personal expression have become a big part of snowboarding. Expect bright and bold colors to be a part of snowboarding culture.

Concepts

Answer the following questions from the information provided in this unit.

1. What is the difference between Alpine and Nordic skiing?

2. When did snowboarding become an Olympic sport?

3. What is a binding? Where is it used? What does it do?

4. What is a trick? Who performs tricks in the snow?

5. How was snowboarding developed? What inspired snowboarding?

Going Places

Culture and Geography

Read the following information about the Switzerland, Swiss culture, climate and cuisine.

Focus on Switzerland, Europe

Switzerland, Europe

Population: 7785,600 (2009 estimate)

Capital: Bern

Largest City: Zurich

Languages: German, French and Italian

Motto: no official motto

Number of islands: 1

Claim to fame: Makes half of the world's watches

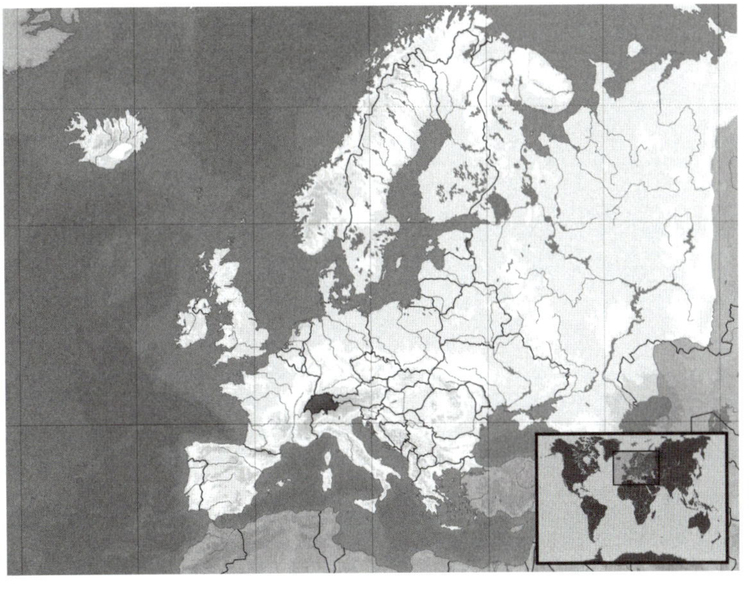

Cuisine

The cuisine of Switzerland is multi-faceted. While some dishes such as fondue are common through the country, each region developed its own gastronomy according to the differences of climate and languages. Traditional Swiss cuisine uses ingredients similar to those in other European countries, as well as unique dairy products and cheeses such as Gruyère or Emmental.

Chocolate had been made in Switzerland since the 18th century but it gained its reputation at the end of the 19th century. Also a breakthrough was the invention of milk chocolate in 1875 by Daniel Peter. The Swiss are the world's largest consumers of chocolate.

The most popular alcoholic drink in Switzerland is wine. Switzerland is notable for the variety of grapes grown because of the large variations in climate. Vineyards have been cultivated in Switzerland since the Roman era, even though certain traces can be found of a more ancient origin.

Climate

Switzerland contains three basic topographical areas: the Swiss Alps on the south, the Central Plateau or Middle Land, and the Jura Mountains on the north. The Swiss climate is generally temperate, but can vary greatly between the localities, from glacial conditions on the mountaintops to the often pleasant near Mediterranean climate at Switzerland's southern tip.

Summers tend to be warm and humid at times with periodic rainfall so they are ideal for pastures and grazing. The winters in the mountains alternate with sun and snow. The lower lands tend to be cloudy and foggy in winter.

- The Alps are a high mountain range running across the central-south of the country, comprising about 60% of the country's total area.
- Among the high valleys of the Swiss Alps many glaciers are found.
- Switzerland has more than 1500 lakes.
- Switzerland contains 6% of Europe's fresh water.
- Lakes and glaciers cover about 6% of the national territory.
- The more populous northern part of the country, comprising about 30% of the country's total area, is called the Middle Land.

Practice Makes Perfect

1. Answer the following questions related to this section. Use complete sentences for your answer.

1) Do Swiss people like chocolate? How do you know?

2) What are the Alps? What are some of the characteristics of the Alps?

3) What is the most popular alcoholic drink in the country? How long has this drink been made there?

4) How many lakes are in Switzerland? How does this affect the amount of freshwater in the country?

5) What are the seasons like in Switzerland?

2. Match the following words from the previous section to the definition that best matches. Draw a line to connect the matching pairs.

1) Freshwater •	• A) Large mass of ice
2) Plateau •	• B) Water with no salt
3) Glacier •	• C) Highland
4) Consumer •	• D) Mild
5) Vineyard •	• E) Crowded
6) Ancient •	• F) Nibble, eat casually
7) Pasture •	• G) Meadow
8) Graze •	• H) Very old
9) Populous •	• I) Winery
10) Temperate •	• J) User

3. Use the following word in a sentence.

1) Pasture: ______________________________

2) Freshwater: ______________________________

3) Ancient: ______________________________

Just Do It

Verbs are the parts of speech that indicate action. Phrasal verbs are two-word verbs, prepositional verbs or two verbs used together. Review the two phrasal verbs below.

To talk someone into something

- To convince someone to do something

EXAMPLE:

- I talked my mother into buying me a puppy.

To run into someone

- To unexpectedly see someone in a public place

EXAMPLE:

- I ran into my former teacher at the store.

UNIT 3

Fore!

Unit Goals

- Build vocabulary and conversation skills for resort sports
- Practice practical resort-specific English
- Learn about the gear and accessories necessary for resort golfing
- Profile golf
- Profile Hainan, China, Haianese cuisine and culture

Vocabulary

- Golf club (equipment)
- Golf tee
- Country club / golf club (place or location to play golf)
- Course
- Strokes (number of times one hits the ball)
- Cleats / golf shoes
- Water hazard
- Caddy
- Sand trap
- Fuzzy
- Incongruous
- Staggering
- Putting green
- Rattan
- Lush
- Bourgeois
- Predominant
- Free range
- Marinade
- Fundamental

Let's Get Started

Translate these common questions relating to golfing. Resort staff would ask some questions, and guests would ask others. In the blank provided, write the letter "S" for staff or the letter "G" for guest, indicating who would ask the question.

1. Will you rent clubs today? ____
2. What is the green fee? ____
3. Is this a private course? ____
4. Would you like a single glove or a pair? ____
5. How much does a lesson cost at the club? ____
6. Did you land in the sand trap today? ____
7. Can I get an earlier tee time? ____
8. Does this resort have a driving range? ____
9. Is there room to work in a single? ____
10. Would you have a 9 iron I can use? ____

Conversation I

Seung Jae: So, Ms. Marie, what's your handicap?

Dawn: What? I'm not handicapped. How could you say that?

Seung Jae: Well, I guess you answered my next question: do you play golf?

Dawn: Ah, I see. That must be a golf term I'm not familiar with. Honestly, when it comes to golf, I don't know much.

Seung Jae: There is not time like the present to start to learn. And here at the resort, we have everything you need to be successful on the green.

Dawn: On the what?

Seung Jae: Oh, dear, I really think that I should schedule a lesson with one of our professionals. What do you think about that?

Dawn: Sounds great. Actually, I was going to ask you about more resort activities to try today.

Seung Jae: I'll schedule a lesson at the driving range. That's the place where you can practice your swing before going to the actual golf course.

Dawn: Great. I am looking forward to this.

Conversation II

Seung Jae: Welcome to the Pro Shop. How can I help you today?

Dawn: I should buy some golfing gloves. I have my first lesson today, and I want to arrive ready.

Seung Jae: First things first; let's measure your hand. We should determine if you are a "regular" or "cadet." A regular fit suits a hand with long fingers and a narrow palm, while a cadet fit is better for a hand with shorter fingers and a wider palm.

Dawn: I think I'm a regular fit.

Seung Jae: Yes, I would agree. Now, let's measure the distance between the base of your palm and the tip of your middle finger. This is how we get the size. (He measures her.) Looks like you're a size small.

Dawn: So, do I need one glove or two? I saw people wearing only one glove. Why is that?

Seung Jae: If you are a right-handed golfer, then you buy a glove for the left hand. If you are a left-handed golfer, then the glove is for your right hand. That is the hand you use to grip the club. Some people chose to wear two gloves, but it's really a personal choice.

Dawn: Let me try on a pair and see how they feel. Do they come in more colors?

Seung Jae: Yes, they come in many colors, but really the material is more important than the color. We have synthetic, leather and thermal. I, however, recommend leather.

Dawn: I'll trust your opinion. After all, this is my first time.

Conversation III

Dawn: Hello, Seung Jae. How are you?

Seung Jae: I'm very well. It's a beautiful day. What will you do?

Dawn: I have a tee-time at noon. The golf club booked me with a group today. It's my first time on the resort course.

Seung Jae: Don't forget your basic golf etiquette; never swing your club towards another person. Also, remember to have a decent pace of play. While most people enjoy a game of golf, they don't want it to last all day.

Dawn: It's ok if I am a little slow though, right?

Seung Jae: Just remember that if you take 120 shots in a game and take 30 extra seconds per shot, that's adding an extra hour to the game.

Dawn: Ahhh, I understand. If I am not mistaken, being quiet is important, right?

Seung Jae: Yes, it's essential. Golf requires focus and concentration. Any loud noises can be distracting.

Dawn: There seems to be so many rules. I just want to have a good time.

Seung Jae: You will have an excellent time. Just relax and enjoy. That's what golf at the resort is all about.

Conversation IV

Seung Jae: How was your first game, Ms. Marie?

Dawn: I'm exhausted. I had to carry that huge golf bag across the entire course. It was torture.

Seung Jae: That might be my fault. I think I forgot to tell you about caddies and carts.

Dawn: Tell me more. This sounds promising.

Seung Jae: We have caddy service here at the resort. A caddy is someone that carries the bag for you. It takes a lot of the work out of golf. All of our caddies are professionals. They know everything about the game and can really help you out.

Dawn: Why didn't you tell me? I really could have used a few pointers and tips today.

Seung Jae: I might be able to make it up to you. We also have golf cart services. A cart is a very small, motorized vehicle that will transport you from hole to hole around the course.

Dawn: Aren't the carts noisy? I thought being quiet was important?

Seung Jae: All of our carts are powered with batteries; they're electric, and silent.

Well Played

Resort guests sometimes vacation in order to relax and participate in recreational activities. Review the following information about resort sports.

Golfing

At one time, golf was considered a sport for the aging; slow and boring. Now, golf has become one of the fastest growing pastimes, for the young and old. A day at the resort golf course can mean fresh air. Golf is a precision club-and-ball sport, in which competing players, using many types of clubs, attempt to hit balls into each hole on a golf course while employing the fewest number of strokes. Golf is one of the few ball games that do not require a standardized playing area. Instead, the game is played on golf "courses", each of which features a unique design, although courses typically consist of either nine or 18 holes.

In 2005, Golf Digest calculated that the countries with most golf courses per capita, starting with the best endowed were: Scotland, New Zealand, Australia, Republic of Ireland, Northern Ireland, Canada, Wales, United States, Sweden, and England (countries with fewer than 500,000 people were excluded). Apart from Sweden, all of these countries have English as the majority language, but the number of courses in non-English speaking countries is increasing rapidly. The most notable example of this phenomenon is China. The first golf course in the People's Republic of China opened in 1984, but by the end of 2009 there were roughly 600 in the country. By October of 2009, China had plans to build 1,400 public courses over the next five years. Currently, only a small number of China's courses are public.

Concepts

Answer the following questions from the information provided in this unit.

1. What is the objective of a game of golf?

2. How has golf changed in China?

3. What type of person might enjoy visiting a golf resort? Why?

4. What countries are famous for great golfing? Why do you think these places are popular for the game?

5. What locations might make for a successful golf resort? Why?

Culture and Geography

Read the following information about Hainan, Haianese culture, climate and cuisine.

Focus on Hainan, China

Hainan Island, People's Republic of China

Population: 8,640,700 (2010 estimate)

Capital and Largest City: Haikou

Languages: Haianese Chinese, Standard Mandarin and Cantonese as 2nd and 3rd languages

Motto: no official motto

Number of islands: 1

Claim to fame: The 42nd largest island in the world

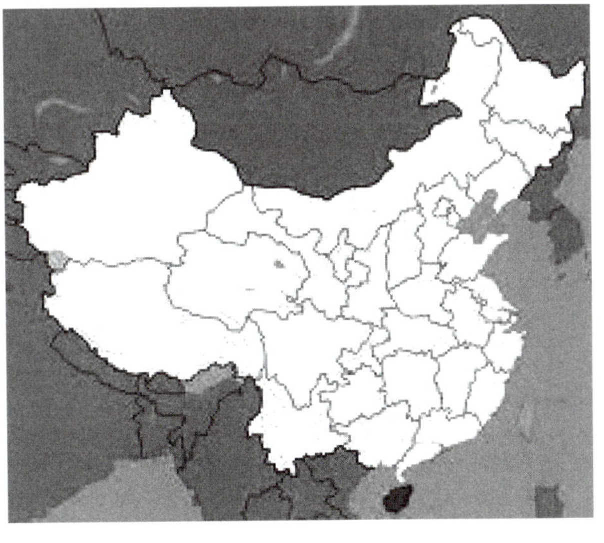

Cuisine

Hainan cuisine is said to be lighter, with mild seasonings. A lot of local taste is mixed with the Han Chinese taste. Seafood predominates the menu, as shrimp, crab, fish and other sea life are widely available.

Wenchang Chicken is a dish known throughout the province of Hainan. Although there are many varieties of this dish, the name is usually used to define a type of small, free-range chicken from Wenchang city, located on the east coast of the province.
Hainan chicken rice is a famous dish in Southeast Asia bearing the region's name. However, whilst many restaurants use chicken fat to quickly add flavor to the dish, the proper local method is to 'marinate' the rice with chicken soup to add fuller flavor.

Climate

Hainan has a tropical moist monsoonal climate.

- Its annual temperature change is less than 15 °C (27.0 °F).
- The coldest months are January and February when the temperatures drop to 16 to 21 °C (61 to 70 °F).
- The hottest months are July and August, and the temperatures are 25 to 29 °C (77 to 84 °F).
- Except for the mountainous regions in the central part of the island, the daily average temperature in Hainan is above 10 °C (50 °F).
- The eastern part of Hainan lies in the path of typhoons.
- 70% of the annual precipitation is derived from typhoons and the summer rainy season.

Practice Makes Perfect

1. Answer the following questions related to this section. Use complete sentences for your answer.

1) Why is seafood a main staple of the Haianese people?

2) Describe a famous chicken dish from Hainan.

3) How much of Hainan's rain comes from the monsoon season? What does this mean for the other months of the year?

4) What is Haianese cuisine like?

5) What are the seasons like in Hainan? How many seasons are there? When is the best time to visit Hainan?

2. Match the following words from the previous section to the definition that best matches. Draw a line to connect the matching pairs.

1) Fuzzy •	• A) Soak
2) Incongruous •	• B) Furry
3) Staggering •	• C) Prevail
4) Stroke •	• D) Amazing
5) Rattan •	• E) Verdant
6) Lush •	• F) Wicker
7) Bourgeois •	• G) Hit
8) Predominate •	• H) Middle-class
9) Free-range •	• I) Out of place
10) Marinade •	• J) Liberated

3. Use the following word in a sentence.

1) Marinade: ______________________________

2) Rattan: ______________________________

3) Free-range: ______________________________

Just Do It

Verbs are the parts of speech that indicate action. Phrasal verbs are two-word verbs, prepositional verbs or two verbs used together. Review the two phrasal verbs below.

To live something down

- To overcome the shame or embarrassment of something

EXAMPLE:

- I made a fool of myself and I will never live it down.

To water something down

- To dilute something, not always with water

EXAMPLE:

- This juice doesn't taste very good: it's watered down.

UNIT 4 Dive in

Unit Goals

- Build vocabulary and conversation skills for resort sports
- Practice practical resort-specific English
- Learn about the gear and accessories necessary for scuba diving and snorkeling
- Profile scuba diving and snorkeling in the Philippines

Vocabulary

- Ray
- To cross one's fingers
- Visibility
- Certification
- Corrective
- To rent
- High–pressure
- Camera housing
- Nocturnal
- To disrupt
- Macro
- Marine sanctuary
- Cuisine
- To evolve
- To adapt
- Robust
- Wreck
- Mild
- Maritime
- Distinctively

Let's Get Started

Translate these common questions relating to scuba diving and snorkeling. Resort staff would ask some questions, and guests would ask others. In the blank provided, write the letter "S" for staff or the letter "G" for guest, indicating who would ask the question.

1. Are you scuba certified? ____

2. Do you have your own snorkeling gear? ____

3. Did you want to dive with us during your vacation? ____

4. Do these boots come in a size 8? ____

5. Do you have a mask with vision correction? ____

6. What time does the dive boat leave in the morning? ____

7. When would you like to schedule your dive? ____

8. Can I get you information on a dive package? ____

9. Where is the dive shop located? ____

10. How much is a single tank dive? ____

Conversation I

Seung Jae: Hello, Ms. Marie.

Dawn: Good morning. How are you?

Seung Jae: I am well. It's rather early for you. Where are you headed this morning?

Dawn: I'm going diving. The early bird gets the worm, right?

Seung Jae: Well, in your case, the early diver sees the best fish!

Dawn: I hope so. I want to spot a ray this morning.

Seung Jae: What is a ray?

Dawn: Really? You don't know? It's a huge, flat marine animal, with a tail. They seem to float when they swim.

Seung Jae: Oh, yes, yes. I know what you mean. I hope your wish comes true.

Dawn: Let's keep our fingers crossed. I'll let you know when I get back.

Conversation II

Seung Jae: Dawn! How was your dive?

Dawn: It was simply fantastic! I say an Eagle Ray, a giant sea turtle, and tons of macro life.

Seung Jae: Wow, I am impressed. I have only been snorkeling. Maybe I should try diving.

Dawn: If you have the time to enjoy it, you should try. You live so close to such great diving. The visibility in the water is excellent.

Seung Jae: How far can you see?

Dawn: At about 10-12 meters down I can see about 35-40 meters.

Seung Jae: Seriously? I had no idea.

Dawn: Well, now you do. Are you tempted to try?

Seung Jae: I am, but don't I need a certification?

Dawn: Sure. You should be certified as an "open water" diver. If you want to try diving first, many organizations will offer a discovery course. You learn the basics, enjoy one dive and then you decide it's your cup of tea.

Seung Jae: Sounds perfect. Maybe you can be my dive-buddy next time.

Conversation III

Seung Jae: Ms. Marie, how are you? Are you going diving again?

Dawn: Yes, but I need some help.

Seung Jae: How can I assist you?

Dawn: I need a corrected mask. I usually wear contact lenses, but they are uncomfortable to wear when I dive. I should try to find a mask that is made with a corrective lens instead.

Seung Jae: Why don't I call the dive shop and see if they have one for you?

Dawn: That sounds great. Can you ask if I can rent one? I would prefer to rent it, rather than buy it.

Seung Jae: Of course I can. Wait just one moment. (He makes a phone call.)

Dawn: What did they tell you?

Seung Jae: They have a mask for you. You can rent it for the day.

Dawn: How much will that cost?

Seung Jae: It's only 50 pesos more than the regular mask. It's a great deal, if it means you will actually be able to see.

Conversation IV

Seung Jae: It's too late to dive. Where are you headed for with your gear at this hour?

Dawn: It's never too late to dive; it's just early enough for night diving!

Seung Jae: You can dive at night, too?

Dawn: Sure, and different animals are out in the day and in the night. It is yet another world at night.

Seung Jae: How can you possibly see anything? There is no sunlight, and the moonlight isn't bright enough.

Dawn: Actually the moonlight does affect a night dive, but not nearly as much as the sunlight. We use flashlights that are waterproof and specially designed for high-pressure environments, like diving.

Seung Jae: Wow, there seems to be so much that I don't know. Just don't tell me you can take pictures at night, too.

Dawn: Actually, you can take pictures at night. Again, we use a special camera, lens, housing for the camera and flash.

Seung Jae: Now, I must learn to dive. I have always wanted to know about the secret nocturnal activities of the underwater world.

Dawn: Just remember never to point the light directly at the fish. Light during the night confuses them, and can disrupt the cycle of life.

Well Played

Resort guests sometimes vacation in order to relax and participate in recreational activities. Review the following information about resort sports.

Scuba Diving

Scuba diving is a form of underwater diving in which a diver uses a scuba set to breathe underwater for recreation, commercial or industrial reasons. The term SCUBA, an acronym for Self-Contained Underwater Breathing Apparatus, arose during World War II, and originally referred to United States combat frogmen's oxygen rebreathers, developed by Dr. Christian Lambertsen for underwater warfare. The word SCUBA began as an acronym, but it is now usually thought of as a regular word – scuba. It has become acceptable to refer to "scuba equipment" or "scuba apparatus".

Resort guests flock to sandy white beaches and coral coves to discover the wonders of an underwater world. Scuba diving is offered at resorts worldwide, and is a popular hobby and vacation pastime for people of all nationalities. Scuba diving is a resort activity, which requires certification in order to participate in. Some resorts may offer certification courses for their guests, while others require previous certification for participation.

According to a 1970 North American study, diving was 96 times more dangerous than driving an automobile. According to a 2000 Japanese study, every hour of recreational diving is 36 to 62 times riskier than automobile driving.

Snorkeling

Snorkeling is similar to scuba inasmuch as a swimmer can remain under the water for extended periods of time. When snorkeling, a resort guest will remain at the surface of the water, and use only a mask, snorkel and fins to navigate the underwater world. The same mask, snorkel and fins used for scuba diving are used for snorkeling.

Snorkeling is a great way to view underwater life because many plants and animals need sunlight to survive. Therefore, there is abundant life near the ocean's surface. Anyone can snorkel and no certification is required. Many times, a snorkeling trip may be arranged with a diving trip. Dive boats often carry snorkeling passengers to remote locations for a small fee.

Snorkel Gear Diagram

Scuba Gear Diagram

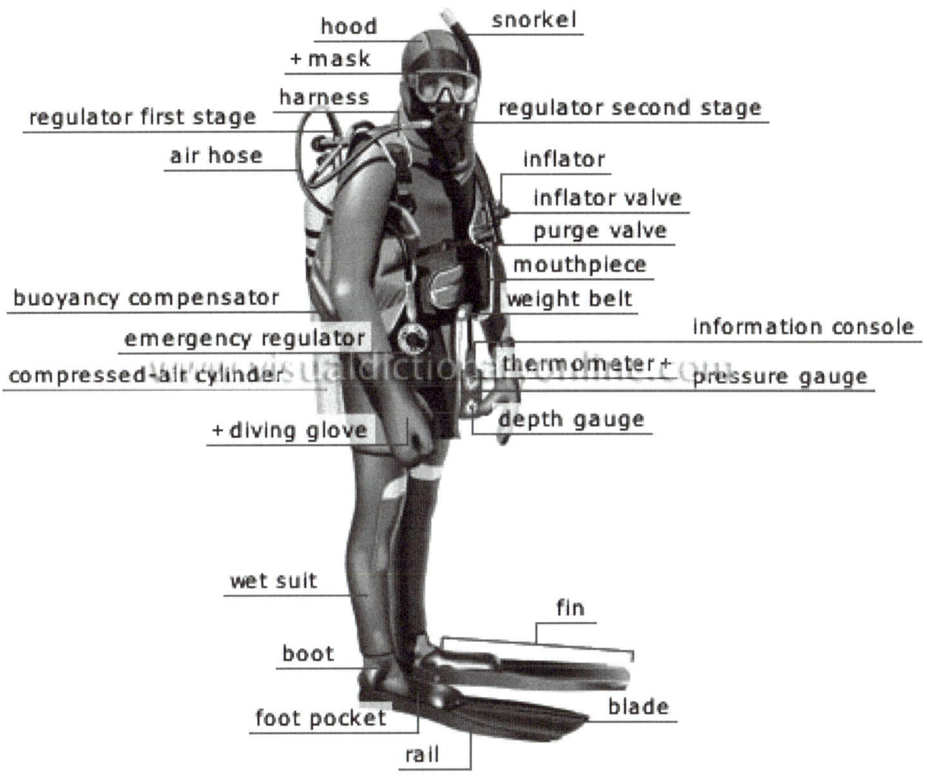

Scuba Diving Gear Translation

Translate each of the following words. Use a dictionary if you are unsure and refer to the diagram for help.

1. Mask ________

2. Snorkel ________

3. arness ________

4. Air hose ________

5. Mouth piece ________

6. Weight belt ________

7. Buoyancy control device (BCD) ________

8. Diving glove ________

9. Boot ________

10. Fin ________

Concepts

Answer the following questions from the information provided in this unit.

1. What is the difference between scuba diving and snorkeling?

2. If a resort guest wants to scuba dive, what should he or she do first?

3. Which gear is used for both scuba diving and snorkeling?

4. Which activity might you suggest to a resort guest if he or she has limited time to spend in the water?

5. Why do people choose to learn to scuba dive or snorkel? What might they see?

Going Places

Culture and Geography

Read the following information about the Philippines, Filipino culture, climate and cuisine.

Focus on the Philippines

Republic of the Philippines

Population: 93,000,000 (2009 estimate)

Capital City: Manila

Largest City: Quezon City

Languages: Filipino, based on Tagalog, English

Motto: For God, people, nature and country

Number of islands: 7,107

Claim to fame: World's 12th most populous country

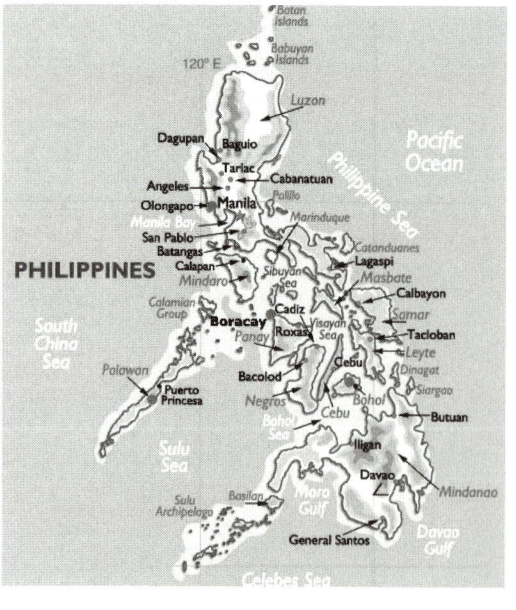

Climate

The Philippines has a tropical maritime climate and is usually hot and humid. There are three seasons: the hot dry season or summer from March to May; the rainy season from June to November; the cool dry season from December to February. The southwest monsoon is from May to October and is known as the Habagat. The dry winds of the northeast monsoon last from November to April. Temperatures usually range from 21°C (70°F) to 32°C (90°F) although it can get cooler or hotter depending on the season. The coolest month is January; the warmest is May.

Cuisine

Philippine cuisine has evolved over several centuries from its Malayo-Polynesian origins to become a mixed cuisine with many Hispanic, Chinese, American, and other Asian influences that have been adapted to local ingredients and the Filipino palate to create distinctively Filipino dishes. Dishes range from the very simple, like a meal of fried salted fish and rice, to the elaborate, such as the paellas and cocidos created for fiestas. Some common local ingredients used in cooking are coconuts, saba (a kind of short wide plantain), mangoes, milkfish, and fish sauce. Filipino taste buds tend to favor robust flavors but the cuisine is not as spicy as other Asian countries.

Unlike many of their Asian counterparts, Filipinos do not eat with chopsticks; they use western cutlery. However, possibly due to rice being the primary staple food and the popularity of a large number of stews and main dishes with broth in Philippine cuisine, the main pairing of utensils seen at the Filipino dining table is that of spoon and fork, not knife and fork. The traditional way of eating with the hands is seen more often in less urbanized areas.

Practice Makes Perfect

1. Answer the following questions related to this article. Use complete sentences for your answer.

1) What is the population of the Philippines? What record does the Philippines hold in terms of population?

2) What is unique about Filipino eating culture? How is it different from Korea, Japan and China?

3) When is a monsoon most likely to hot the Philippines?

4) What is traditional or typical Filipino food like? What should a resort guest expect?

5) What are the seasons like in the Philippines? How many seasons are there? What is the average temperature? When is the best time to visit the Philippines?

2. Match the following words from the previous article to the definition that best matches. Draw a line to connect the matching pairs.

1) Macro •	• A) Develop
2) Marine sanctuary •	• B) Food
3) Cuisine •	• C) Refuge for sea plants and animals
4) Evolve •	• D) Large-scale
5) Adapt •	• E) Remains
6) Robust •	• F) Calm
7) Wreck •	• G) Full-bodied
8) Mild •	• H) Uniquely
9) Maritime •	• I) Change
10) Distinctively •	• J) Naval

3. Use the following word in a sentence.

1) Robust: ______________________________

2) Macro: ______________________________

3) Maritime: ______________________________

Just Do It

Verbs are the parts of speech that indicate action. Phrasal verbs are two-word verbs, prepositional verbs or two verbs used together. Review the two phrasal verbs below.

To rope something off

- To isolate an area with a rope

EXAMPLE:

- The accident site was roped off.

To clock in / to clock out

- To record one's arrival or departure time, usually associated with work

EXAMPLE:

- What time did she clock in? Was she late?

UNIT 5 The Sky's the Limit

Unit Goals

- Build vocabulary and conversation skills for resort sports
- Practice practical resort-specific English
- Learn about the gear and accessories necessary for parasailing
- Profile parasailing in Thailand

Vocabulary

- To arrange
- Adrenalin
- Opposite
- Same time, same place
- Deal
- To secure
- Seasick
- Waterproof
- Sunscreen
- To be on the ball
- Quintessential
- Horde
- Immensely
- High-rise
- Sloping
- Pervade
- Bender
- Abruptly
- Domestically
- Fundamental

Let's Get Started

Translate these common questions relating to parasailing. Resort staff would ask some questions, and guests would ask others. In the blank provided, write the letter "S" for staff or the letter "G" for guest, indicating who would ask the question.

1. Have you been parasailing before? ____

2. Do you prefer a morning or afternoon appointment? ____

3. Where can I find information about parasailing? ____

4. Is it safe? ____

5. Has this company had any accidents? ____

6. Would you like to go alone, or with a friend? ____

7. How long will my ride last? ____

8. How much do you weigh? ____

9. Where is the departure point for parasailing? ____

10. We are a group of 5. Can we get a discount? ____

Conversation I

Seung Jae: Now that you have been diving, what other sports have you considered enjoying here at the resort?

Dawn: I thought about parasailing, but I am scared of heights. I guess I'm just not sure yet.

Seung Jae: That's understandable. But I have to say that parasailing certainly gives you the best view of the resort property. I've been there and it's beautiful.

Dawn: You went? What was it like? Was it scary?

Seung Jae: I was nervous at first, but the tour operator explained everything to me. When he was finished teaching me, I was ready.

Dawn: Wow. What did you see? What was it like?

Seung Jae: Well, Ms. Marie, it's not all about what you see, but also what you feel. It's the closest I have ever come to flying. I felt free.

Dawn: I always say if I could be an animal, I would be a bird. I guess then I couldn't be scared of heights. Have you ever heard of a bird being scared to fly?

Seung Jae: No. Are you kidding? This is all the more reason to try. I can call the tour operator for you and schedule an appointment to check it out, if you would like.

Dawn: Okay! Do it. Now, there is no going back!

Conversation II

Seung Jae: Welcome to Parasailing Paradise. How can we help you?

Dawn: I would like to learn more about parasailing, but I have to admit; I am a little nervous.

Seung Jae: Let me ease your fears. First and foremost, we have a 100% safety rating; no injuries or accidents.

Dawn: Actually, that does help. How much will one trip cost?

Seung Jae: The price depends on the amount of time you would like to spend in the air. It ranges from 400-1000 baht for 5-30 minutes.

Dawn: So, I have options? If I pay for 20 minutes, but I want to come down early, can I get a refund?

Seung Jae: We can arrange for you to pay after the trip. So, don't worry about a refund. We only charge for what you do.

Dawn: Great. What about the weather? Is today a good day?

Seung Jae: Honestly, early mornings are best, when the air is a little cooler and before the clouds roll in. We can book you for tomorrow morning, if you'd like.

Dawn: Actually, yes, I am ready. I can feel the adrenalin already. Let's book it for tomorrow morning at 9 am.

Seung Jae: Okay, Ms. Marie. I'll see you tomorrow. Thanks for stopping by.

Conversation III

Dawn: Wow. That was great. I can't believe how beautiful the beach is here. I never would have known if I hadn't gone parasailing.

Seung Jae: That's the general opinion when someone finishes his or her first ride.

Dawn: What do you mean, 'first ride'?

Seung Jae: Well, one ride usually turns into two or three. It's just so beautiful up there; it's hard to get enough of the Thai scenery.

Dawn: If I go again, can we depart from the opposite side of the bay? I would like to check out a different area.

Seung Jae: Hooked already, Ms. Marie? Sure. You can depart from the opposite side of the bay, if you wish.

Dawn: Tomorrow morning then? Same time, same place?

Seung Jae: You've got it.

Dawn: But for three trips, could I get a discount?

Seung Jae: I think I can work out a deal for you; a package of three trips for 20% off.

Dawn: Sold.

Conversation IV

Seung Jae: How did you sleep last night? Ready for the big ride?

Dawn: Ready or not, I'm going!

Seung Jae: You'll be fine; just don't forget to secure your sunglasses before you takeoff. It would be a shame to lose them.

Dawn: You're right. I never thought of that. Any more helpful tips?

Seung Jae: Well, do you get seasick? The boat ride before you go up can be rough, so you might want to take some medicine to avoid feeling seasick.

Dawn: Where can I get it? I think I need some.

Seung Jae: It's available in the resort pharmacy. Also, you might want to pick up a single-use waterproof camera before you go out. You may end up in the water. It's better to just leave your camera on the boat.

Dawn: Again, you're on the ball. Look's like I'm ready.

Seung Jae: You already applied sunscreen? Don't even think about going up without sunscreen. The sun is stronger than it feels.

Well Played

Resort guests sometimes vacation in order to relax and participate in recreational activities. Review the following information about resort sports.

Parasailing

Parasailing has become a resort activity that attracts visitors who seek a bird's eye view of the beach. Parasailing is a sport passengers are strapped into a harness and pulled by a boat. A parachute, attached to the passenger harness, allows the passenger to glide through the air with the greatest of ease.

The world's first working prototype of winch-boat parasailing was tested in 1974 and patented on October 26, 1976. It was commercially available in the mid 80's, after being plagued by numerous accidents. Today, winch-boat parasailing represents more than 90% of all commercial parasailing offered throughout the world. The boat is equipped with a parasail inflation system and hydraulic winch powered by the main drive engine to launch and retrieve the parasailor from the flight deck, usually located in the rear of the boat. Parasailing does not require the passenger to have a certification, but each resort guest should listen carefully to all directions given by the tour operators to ensure a safe experience.

Parasailing Equipment

The Body Harness

Parasailors are strapped to a body harness assembly, which attaches to the parasail canopy, which is connected by rope to a hydraulic winch mounted on the towboat.

The Rigid Chair

Unlike the harness, parasailors are seated in a partially reclined position in a floating chair that encapsulates and secures without straps. The chair is attached to the parasail canopy, which is connected by rope to a hydraulic winch mounted on the towboat.

Canopy Inflation (by hand)

The towboat accelerates while the crewmember holds the canopy and risers lines until the wind is oncoming wind is sufficient to inflate the canopy. The crewmember feeds the canopy and lines out by hand.

Canopy Inflation (mast)

The canopy riser lines are attached to the mast line and hosted up allowing the oncoming wind to inflate the canopy. Once inflated the mast line is lowered and detached from the canopy riser lines.

Harness Liftoff

The towboat then accelerates lifting the parasailor of the flight deck skyward. Once aloft, achieving altitude is similar to beach parasailing. Altitude is controlled by boat speed.

Chair Liftoff

The towboat then accelerates lifting the parasailor of the flight deck skyward. Once aloft, achieving altitude is similar to beach parasailing. Altitude is controlled by boat speed.

Landing

When the flight is finished, the towboat operator engages the hydraulic winch that reels the parasailor to the flight deck without the parasailor steering the canopy. The boat speed must be synchronized with line speed to avoid a rough landing.

Concepts

Answer the following questions from the information provided in this unit.

1. When was parasailing widely available?

2. What is the difference between the body harness and rigged chair approach to parasailing?

3. Why do people parasail? Why is this a good activity for resort-goers?

4. What is the order of events for parasailing?

5. Why is Thailand a good place to experience parasailing?

Going Places

Culture and Geography

Read the following information about Thailand, Thai culture, climate and cuisine.

Focus on Thailand

Kingdom of Thailand

Population: 65,998,436 (2010 estimate)

Capital and Largest City: Bangkok

Languages: Thai

Motto: Unity amongst those uniting brings about success and prosperity

Number of islands: 1,430

Claim to fame: The 50th largest country in the world

Climate

Thailand's climate varies by region, and the following covers just the Bangkok central region and the north and northeast. The peninsular south is less predictable and more subject to change. The seasons are determined by the "monsoons", which are consistent wind patterns that change at different times of the year due to the differences between land and sea temperatures and pressures. There are three distinct seasons in Thailand.

November thru February – Dry, "Cool" Season

Winds are predominantly from the north when this season starts. Daytime high temperatures are between 30-35 C (85-95 F), humidity of 50% to 60%. Every day is a sunny day. The ground will still be saturated in many places in November due to the previous rainy season.

March thru June – Hot Season

Travelers unaccustomed to the heat should not arrive in this period. Even the Thais have problems in the hottest spells. Temperatures can soar to 40 C (105 F) on the hottest days, and at night the humidity rises.

July thru October – Rainy Season

It rarely rains for more than an hour at a time. The mornings are usually sunny, but a thunderstorm can come towards the late afternoon or at night. This usually starts in late July or August, but by September there is a thunderstorm on most days, often resulting in flooded streets but cooler nighttime temperatures. This season usually ends abruptly in late October when the winds suddenly change to the north.

Cuisine

In Thailand, food forms a central part of any social occasions—and vice versa. That is, food often becomes the social occasion in itself, or reason to celebrate. Thai cuisine blends five fundamental tastes: sweet, spicy, sour, bitter and salty. Some common ingredients used in Thai cuisine include garlic, chilies, lime juice, lemon grass, and fish sauce.

The staple food in Thailand is rice, particularly jasmine variety rice, which is included in almost every meal. Thailand is the world's largest exporter of rice, and Thais domestically consume over 100 kg of milled rice per person per year. Over 5000 varieties of rice from Thailand are preserved in the rice gene bank of the International Rice Research Institute (IRRI), based in the Philippines. The king of Thailand is the official patron of IRRI.

Although the Chinese brought chopsticks to Thailand long ago, today most Thais prefer to use Western cutlery, though in their own special way. Thai cutlery generally consists of a fork and large spoon. The spoon is held in the right hand and used in place of a knife.

A word of warning: Thais have mastered spice; hot means HOT. Start slow with Thai spice and work your way up from there.

Practice Makes Perfect

1. Answer the following questions related to this section. Use complete sentences for your answer.

1) Which season is Thailand in the month of August? What would it be like to visit a Thai resort at this time?

2) How many varieties of Thai rice are there? How are they tracked?

3) Which five fundamental tastes does Thai cuisine incorporate?

4) What is Thai food like? Why should resorts guest be careful?

5) What are the seasons like in Thailand? How many seasons are there? When is the best time to visit Thailand?

2. Match the following words from the previous section to the definition that best matches. Draw a line to connect the matching pairs.

1) Quintessential •	• A) Inclined
2) Horde •	• B) Tall
3) Immensely •	• C) Enormously
4) High-rise •	• D) Crowd
5) Sloping •	• E) Ideal
6) Pervade •	• F) Basically
7) Bender •	• G) Nationally
8) Abruptly •	• H) Suddenly
9) Domestically •	• I) Binge
10) Fundamentally •	• J) Pass through

3. Use the following word in a sentence.

1) Bender: ______________________________

2) Domestically: ______________________________

3) High-rise: ______________________________

Just Do It

Verbs are the parts of speech that indicate action. Phrasal verbs are two-word verbs, prepositional verbs or two verbs used together. Review the two phrasal verbs below.

To read something off

- To read aloud from a list

EXAMPLE:

- The girl read off the groceries she was to buy.

To cue someone in

- To indicate to someone that a specific time has come or to tell them information

EXAMPLE:

- I don't know what's happening. Somebody cued me in.

UNIT
6

Grand Slam

Unit Goals

- Build vocabulary and conversation skills for resort sports
- Practice practical resort-specific English
- Learn about the gear and accessories necessary for tennis
- Profile tennis
- Profile Bali, Indonesia, Balinese cuisine and culture

Vocabulary

- Opponent
- Singles / doubles
- Spectator
- Tennis court
- Apparel
- Restrictive
- Stockings / pantyhose
- Hollow
- Match
- Racket
- Staple
- Polished
- Restricted
- Consumption
- Status
- Avid
- Humid
- Offshore
- Minor
- Ritual

Let's Get Started

Translate these common questions relating to tennis. Resort staff would ask some questions, and guests would ask others. In the blank provided, write the letter "S" for staff or the letter "G" for guest, indicating who would ask the question.

1. Will you play singles or doubles? ____

2. Can I rent a racket? ____

3. Do you have tennis shoes? ____

4. How much does one match cost? ____

5. Is the price of play included in my resort stay? ____

6. Can you match me with another single for a game, please? ____

7. Who won the match? ____

8. Do you have an appointment on the court? ____

9. What time would you like to play? ____

10. Where are the tennis courts located? ____

Conversation I

Seung Jae: Have you been on the court yet?

Dawn: I'm headed there now.

Seung Jae: Are you playing singles or doubles today?

Dawn: Singles. I found someone to play against, but we don't have enough people to play doubles.

Seung Jae: I understand. Maybe when you get to the tennis court, you will meet another team. Then, you might be able to play a game of doubles.

Dawn: Either way, I am happy to play. It's very bright outside today, though. I hope I can keep my eye on the ball.

Seung Jae: Are we talking about golf or tennis now?

Dawn: Tennis, of course. It never hurts to be able to see what you want to make racket contact with.

Seung Jae: Your point is well taken, Ms. Marie. How long have you been playing tennis?

Dawn: I started when I was three years old.

Seung Jae: So, you must be a professional already.

Dawn: I am hardly a professional, but I really enjoy the game.

Conversation II

Seung Jae: Ms. Marie, can I ask you something?

Dawn: Sure, what is it?

Seung Jae: You told me to play tennis, so I was wondering; how is a tennis game scored? I have never been able to understand the scoring system.

Dawn: Actually, I get this question a lot. It is not as straightforward as basketball or soccer.

Seung Jae: Truth be told, it has been confusing me for years.

Dawn: Well, today is your lucky day. Points are earned each time the serving player hits the ball and the receiving player cannot return it. As long as the serving player hits inside the court, then he or she earns a point.

Seung Jae: How do you know who wins the game?

Dawn: Well, the server's score is always called first. To win a game, a player must win 4 points, with a 2-point lead.

Seung Jae: Wait a minute. You lost me.

Dawn: You need 4 points to win, and you have to win by 2 points, so if your opponent has 3 points, you need a score of 5-3 to win the match.

Conversation III

Seung Jae: So, I guess in tennis, the racket you use is important.

Dawn: Sure. If you are a serious player, you will have a serious racket.

Seung Jae: Well, I bet you have a good racket then.

Dawn: Technically speaking, you hit the ball with the strings, not the racket.

Seung Jae: So, the strings are important, too?

Dawn: Yes. A professional shop should string rackets. It's not a good idea to do it yourself if you are a beginner.

Seung Jae: What about tennis balls? Are there any special kinds?

Dawn: For most players, any fresh can of balls will work just fine.

Seung Jae: So, a properly strung racket, a fresh can of balls and a good backhand swing is that all I need?

Conversation IV

Seung Jae: I have always wondered why women wear skirts to play tennis.

Dawn: Wow, Seung Jae, that has to do with a long history of sports appeal. It all started in the 1860s. For a long time, tennis clothing for women was heavy, tight and restrictive.

Seung Jae: Well, it certainly doesn't sound comfortable.

Dawn: It doesn't look comfortable, either. I saw some old photographs on the Internet. I can't imagine what that would be like.

Seung Jae: Why is white so popular? Do you know?

Dawn: Well, white became popular because it doesn't show when a player has been sweating.

Seung Jae: That makes sense. It's a practical reason.

Dawn: Right, and it wasn't until the 1930s that women quit wearing stockings to play tennis.

Seung Jae: I am happy that times have changed. You might not be so interested in the sport otherwise.

Well Played

Resort guests sometimes vacation in order to relax and participate in recreational activities. Review the following information about resort sports.

Tennis

Resort guests are often couples or families that enjoy playing sports together. Tennis is an active leisure activity that can involve the whole family. Even single resort guests can sign up to play tennis together. Tennis is a sport usually played between two players. This is called 'singles'. Also, it can be played between two teams of two players each. This is knows as doubles. Each player uses a racket to strike a hollow rubber ball, covered with felt, over a net into the opponent's court.

The modern game of tennis originated in the United Kingdom in the late 19th century as "lawn tennis". After its creation, tennis spread throughout the upper-class English-speaking population before spreading around the world. Tennis is an Olympic sport and is played at all levels of society at all ages. The sport can be played by anyone who can hold a racket, including people in wheelchairs.

The rules of tennis have not changed much since the 1890s. A recent addition to professional tennis has been the adoption of electronic review technology coupled with a point challenge system, which allows a player to challenge the umpire's call of a point. Players have unlimited opportunity to challenge, but once three incorrect challenges are made in a set, they cannot challenge again until the next set. Tennis is enjoyed by millions of recreational players and is also a hugely popular worldwide spectator sport.

Concepts

Answer the following questions from the information provided in this unit.

1. Where did tennis originate? What was it originally called?

2. Who can play tennis?

3. What are the two types of tennis called? Why do you think that they have these names?

4. What is the basic equipment used in tennis?

5. What is the most recent change in the rules of tennis? How does this new system work?

Culture and Geography

Read the following information about Hawaii, Hawaiian culture, climate and cuisine.

Focus on Bali, Indonesia

Bali, Indonesia

Population: 3,551,000

Capital and Largest City: Denpasar

Languages: Balinese (commonly called Bahasa Bali), Bahasa Indonesia

Motto: Unity in Diversity

Number of islands: 3

Claim to fame: Each day offerings are given to the gods in front of each house and store.

Cuisine

The staple food of Bali is white, polished rice. The traditional Balinese rice tastes better, but is restricted to a few areas and is now mainly used as a ritual food. Other, less frequently grown varieties are red rice, black rice, sticky rice and a type of dry rice grown in the mountains. Rice consumption averages 0.5 kilo per day in Ball.

Many local vegetables grow in a semi-wild state. These include the leaves of several trees and shrubs, varieties of beans, including soybeans, water spinach, the bulbs and leaves of the cassava plant, sweet potatoes, maize, and trunk of the banana tree, young jackfruits, breadfruits and papayas may also be cooked as vegetables. Foreign low-status; high status foods are rice and meat. Meat is reserved for ritual occasions because it is expensive. Surprisingly, fish plays a minor role as a source of protein. Though the seas surrounding Bali are rich, the Balinese are not avid fishermen, as the sea is considered dangerous and impure.

Climate

Bali is eight degrees below the equator and has a yearly tropical monsoon climate. There is very little change in the average temperatures across the year. The wet season runs from November to March. The coastal areas have high humidity during the wet season. Resort guests will feel sticky and hot a lot of the time. When considering Bali weather and climate, the dry season from June to October is the best time of year to travel. Guests will be greeted with clear skies and warm temperatures.

Surfers have 2 seasons to consider. During the middle of the dry season, July to September, the west coast of Bali is favorable for surfing. While in the wet months, from November to March, the wind turns around and the west side of the island has the better offshore breaks. The month of July is very windy, and while great for the locals to fly their large kites, it can be a bit harsh for guests. This mainly affects the southern coast.

Practice Makes Perfect

1. Answer the following questions related to this section. Use complete sentences for your answer.

1) How much rice is eaten, per person each day, on average, in Bali?

2) When is the best season to visit Bali? Why?

3) How does Bali feel in the wet season? When is the wet season?

4) When is meat mainly eaten? Why?

5) Do the Balinese eat fish? Why or why not?

2. Match the following words from the previous section to the definition that best matches. Draw a line to connect the matching pairs.

1) Staple	A) Devoted
2) Polished	B) Small
3) Restricted	C) Position
4) Consumption	D) Ceremonial
5) Status	E) Rate of eating
6) Avid	F) Refined
7) Humid	G) Limited
8) Offshore	H) Away from the beach
9) Minor	I) Moist
10) Ritual	J) Essential

3. Use the following word in a sentence.

1) Offshore: ______________________________

2) Avid: ______________________________

3) Ritual: ______________________________

Just Do It

Verbs are the parts of speech that indicate action. Phrasal verbs are two-word verbs, prepositional verbs or two verbs used together. Review the two phrasal verbs below.

To account for something

- To explain or give a reason for something

EXAMPLE:

- Can you account for the missing money?

To talk back to someone

- To speak or answer back to someone rudely or with disrespect

EXAMPLE:

- Don't talk back to your teacher.

References

Blow-up Sheep and False Leg Among Items Left in Hotel Rooms. Internet. Accessed Sept. 2010.

Crumly, Bruce. *Most Obnoxious Tourists? The French.* Friday, Jul. 04, 2008. Internet.

Elliott Christopher, Tribune Media Services. Oct. 22 2010.

La Carmina. *Big and fashionable: Plus-sized shopping in Asia.* Jun 7 2010. Internet. Accessed Nov 2010

Mohen, Tanya. *Hotels Take 'LocallyGrown' aLogicalStepBeyond.* October 18, 2010. Internet.

Travel Troubleshooter. www.hotel-assist.com. Internet. Accessed Nov. 2010.

Wikipedia. Internet. Accessed Sept. – Nov. 2010.

저자약력

Myeong-Hee Seong

Ph. D. in English Education, Korea University
Professor, Eulji Univ. Faculty of Liberal Arts

Katie Mae Klemsen

M.A. in International Studies, Monterey Institute of International Studies
Professor, Ajou Univ. Dept. of English Language and Literature

Resort & Sports English

2014년 11월 25일 초판 1쇄 인쇄
2014년 11월 30일 초판 1쇄 발행

지은이 Myeong-Hee Seong
Katie Mae Klemsen
펴낸이 진욱상 · 진성원
펴낸곳 백산출판사
교 정 편집부
본문디자인 박채린
표지디자인 오정은

저자와의 합의하에 인지첩부 생략

등 록 1974년 1월 9일 제1-72호
주 소 서울시 성북구 정릉로 157(백산빌딩 4층)
전 화 02-914-1621/02-917-6240
팩 스 02-912-4438
이메일 editbsp@naver.com
홈페이지 www.ibaeksan.kr

ISBN 979-11-5763-004-2
값 13,000원